SOCIAL KISSING, (

HOW TO GET ON WITH PEOPLE WORLDWIDE

Frederick Marsh

Pen Press

First published in Great Britain by Pen Press
All paper used in the printing of this book has been made from wood
grown in managed, sustainable forests.

ISBN13: 978-1-906710-89-7

Printed and bound in the UK
Pen Press is an imprint of Indepenpress Publishing Limited
25 Eastern Place
Brighton
BN2 1GJ

A catalogue record of this book is available from
the British Library

Cover design by Jacqueline Abromeit

For Muriel

Nepali Proverb

In the land of the blind, close your eyes,
in the land of the lame, walk with a limp.

Corresponding English Proverb

When thou art at Rome,
do as they do at Rome.

Contents

Nepali Proverb

In the land of the blind, close your eyes,
in the land of the lame, walk with a limp.

Corresponding English Proverb

When thou art at Rome,
do as they do at Rome.

Contents

INTRODUCTION AND ACKNOWLEDGEMENTS

Introduction

Who is this book for? It is intended for many different readers. For busy executives and officials with limited time to prepare for visiting foreign countries. For tourists and students to help them to better understand the customs and way of life of people in foreign countries. For those who have either direct or indirect contact with people in other countries, which include those responsible for hosting foreign visitors, design products for export and are responsible for marketing products and services in foreign markets.

There are still many people who think that their good home-bred manners will be universally understood. In our own country we know the language, codes of behaviour and social customs, but once abroad we are immediately faced with unfamiliar situations. Even speaking the foreign language of a country combined with abundant goodwill will not alone guarantee a successful relationship.

People from other countries often have very different cultural backgrounds. It is hoped that this book will provide a useful chart for negotiating the minefield of cultural differences.

How is this book to be read? Each subject is treated as an independent chapter and alphabetically arranged, so that one can dip into the book at any point. Many chapters are cross-referenced.

Even ordinary actions such as speaking on the telephone, making an appointment, greeting people, making gestures, or standing apart or close when in conversation can be misunderstood. Executives should be aware that their management style may be inappropriate in another country, having not only a negative effect but even causing offence.

During a conversation or at meetings we may sense that things are not going well, that our message does not seem to be understood and that a misunderstanding has occurred, but we cannot understand why. During a discussion we feel that our assumptions are not being confirmed, or simply that we do not receive the feedback we are anticipating. This may well be due cultural factors not known to us, this will be the time to pause, and a different style or approach may be called for.

Gestures of friendship too, can be misunderstood. We may be touching when we shouldn't be. Even what may seem to us a typical gesture, such as nodding our head in affirmation or shaking our head to indicate a negative response, may be misinterpreted in some countries. We may be offering gifts to communicate pleasure that are perceived by the recipient to be linked with sorrow.

The way other people work, communicate, negotiate, arrive at decisions, eat and drink, socialise and make friends in other countries, are often very different from those with which we are familiar. Our actions and their reactions may lead to embarrassment to either or both parties. Our actions can lead to failure of a mission, to lost business onto cancelled contracts.

To be able to communicate successfully with a person from another country or culture it is essential to focus one's antennae and in particular fine-tune those of one's senses which are in command of sight and sound.

Some time ago a university invited me to give a light hearted after-dinner speech which was to deal with the kind of pitfalls executives might encounter when visiting a foreign country. By that time I had visited some 80 countries and I described my experiences and one of the many faux pas I had committed. I told them that during a lecture at an institute in a West African country I had spoken about the nature of culture, and suggested that one could compare it with an iceberg. I went on to say that to most people only a very small part of culture is visible. This visible part of which they are almost always aware included food, cooking, dress, fine arts, literature, games, folk dancing and popular music. The invisible part of which most people are not consciously aware included eye contact, body language, roles in relation to status by age, sex and class, patterns of superior / subordinate relations, relationship to animals, and many, many others. My reason for suggesting that the nature of culture is like an iceberg was that, only one tenth is visible and the major part is out of sight below the surface. I showed a picture of an iceberg. I then noticed that the message did not get through and something was wrong. It was soon made clear to me that the cause of this was the iceberg metaphor. In West Africa people are not aware of icebergs. If one wishes to illustrate that a very small part of something is visible and the major part invisible one has to use a more familiar and familiar concept, in this case a hippopotamus. An imagine of a hippo in water shows that only a part of its skull, its eyes, ears and nostril are visible, while most of its body is submerged.

Since then I have read many books on the subject of cross-cultural relations and discussed my experiences with many fellow business travellers, officials and tourists, often while waiting in airport lounges and on long intercontinental flights. These conversations showed that although there is a wealth of published information, it is not generally available in a compact, readable and entertaining format which then led me to write this book.

I have also learned that while it is neither easy and probably not practical to learn the language of each and every country one visits, nevertheless it is always possible to learn to say 'thank you' in other languages. The ability just to say 'thank you' has always stood me in good stead.

Experienced travellers suggest that factors leading to any successful cross-cultural relationship are *tolerance*, *flexibility* and *co-operation*. In this context I am sometimes asked whether there is one, just one single piece of advice as to what one can do when one realises that one has made a minor or even a monumental blunder. My suggestion is to smile sweetly, but not to let this smile develop into an idiotic grin. It may be a simplistic answer but it has got me out of many a tight corner.

Throughout this book I have endeavoured to use gender-neutral words like business executive. However where I have used the word man it also includes woman, as do the pronouns — he or his.

Acknowledgements

I am indebted to the many organisations which not only opened my eyes and stimulated my interest in intercultural relations but also provided the opportunities to obtain practical experience of inter-cultural relations. My work with them was starting point for writing this book. These organisations include: the United Nations Agency — International Trade Centre/UNCTAD/WTO Geneva, Switzerland; PRODEC — Programme for Development Co-operation, Helsinki School of Economics, Finland; Universita Commerciale Luigi Bocconi / University Bocconi, Milan, Italy; H.O.P.E — Hellenic Organisation for the Promotion of Export, Athens, Greece; MPEDA — The Marine Products Export Development Agency, Cochin, India; Federation of Nepalese Chambers of Commerce and Industry, Kathmandu, Nepal; Eastern and Southern African Management Institute, Arusha, Tanzania; Ministry of Foreign Trade of Ethiopia, Addis Ababa, Ethiopia; CBI — Centre for Promotion of Imports from Developing countries), Netherlands; ZDS — Zentral Fachschule der Deutschen Suesswarenwirtschaft e.V., Solingen, Germany; ESCAP — UN Economic and Social Commission for Asia and the Pacific, Bangkok, Thailand; Ministry of Trade, Hanoi and Ho Chi Minh City, Vietnam; Watt Publishing Company, Chicago, USA the organisers of Pet Food Forums and Conferences; United States of America, Department of Commerce, Washington DC, USA; FEDIAF — European Pet Food Industry Federation, Brussels, Belgium; Seminars and conferences organised by the China Great Wall Exhibition Company, Beijing, China; and by LENEXPO, St. Petersburg, Russia. Also of considerable assistance were projects undertaken for British clients such as — the Reed Travel Group of Dunstable, Croner Publications of Kingston-upon-Thames, the University of Strathclyde in Glasgow and the University of Leeds.

Furthermore of great help were my colleagues at The World Air Education Organisation and at the FAI (Fédération Aéronautique

Internationale — the World Air Sports Federation), Lausanne, Switzerland. On occasions they were puzzled when I asked them to spell, usually on corners of committee papers an imitation of natural sounds (onomatopoeia) associated with the barking of dogs and miaowing of cats. This may help to explain why some of them, including Madame Balesi-Rousseau of France and Mrs Kyung O Kim of Korea sometimes moved their chairs slightly away from me at board meetings. I also noted the raised eyebrows of my British colleagues when I wandered in deep conversation with my Chinese counterpart, a three star Air Force General, hand-in-hand, across an airfield. Likewise my colleagues at Europe Air Sport who expressed concern about my sexual orientation when I enquired about the congratulatory kissing etiquette among male participants at an international parachuting championship.

I would like to thank the many government officials, business executives and editors of newspapers and magazines for their advice and guidance when discussing with them cultural issues as part of international trade relations.

Some of the contents of this book have been presented at seminars, conferences and workshops and I would like to express my appreciation to the participants for their constructive comments.

I would particularly like to express my appreciation and thanks to my editor, Catriona Rose Watson.

Finally I would like to thank my wife Muriel. She accompanied me on a number of overseas missions. On several of these she was volunteered, or rather dropped in the deep end, as seminar projectionist and in various other roles, all of which she performed with her natural inimitable panache and style. This book is dedicated to her for all her help and encouragement with love and appreciation.

Frederick Marsh

ACHIEVEMENTS

In order to recognise and evaluate effectively manifestations of personal achievement in another country, it is necessary to know and recognise status symbols in one's own country.

There are numerous different manifestations and indicators of achievement. In many Western culture countries visible indicators include location within an office block of the office of the person one is visiting, the presence of a personal assistant or secretary, the size of the office, office furniture and embellishments, even size of office desk may be an indicator of achievement and status. Other indicators might include manner of speech and personal appearance including clothing and accessories. Some other pointers may only become apparent during subsequent conversation, such as pursuit of sports as well as other social interests, type of car owned and membership of clubs.

In some societies achievement through one's own effort is valued more highly than ostensible achievement due to family reputation or patronage.

It is important to be aware that in other counties and among other social classes very different norms apply and therefore to use one's own culture norms as a standard may result in quite misleading perceptions.

Also read

- Links and connections
- Sense of time
- Status symbols
- Verbal and visual presentations

ADVERTISING

Translating advertising copy and slogans is not just a question of translating and transposing words into a foreign language. The skill lies in producing copy which still retains the feel of the original while appealing to the reader who may be living in a completely different cultural environment. Even photographs and illustrations can be misunderstood.

In addition every language has its own typographical style and conventions including diacritical marks, punctuation and capital letters. In some countries sales and promotional brochures and related material may require to be produced to be read from right to left or vertically instead of horizontally.

There are a number of languages which have an alphabet and ways of speaking which make the reading of words in English difficult and sometime almost impossible. German-speakers find it difficult to pronounce the English letter W, as in 'white', 'winter' or 'wood'; likewise in France where words or names starting with the English letter H as in 'hat', 'horse' or 'hotel' can cause problems. This is important, particularly if potential customers or buyers cannot pronounce the name of the product they wish to buy.

Not only can photographs and illustrations be misunderstood in another culture, they can transmit a completely different message from the one intended, therefore every aspect of a photograph or illustration requires to be checked before it is published in another country. There are some countries where details such as just a few small lines on a person's face may indicate a particular clan or tribe, or an additional fold in a woman's dress may identify a woman belonging to a particular social class or caste, in both cases this may lead to a misinterpretation of the intended message.

There are many reported cases of how companies made mistakes either with text copy or illustrations when trying to promote their products in countries where a different language is spoken. Whilst some may well be amusing they can result in monetary damage to company and product.

Baby food packaging in most regions of the world usually feature images of cheerful babies together with text describing package contents. Some time ago a baby food manufacturer who was marketing his products in countries where the literacy level was low, in this instance in Africa, decided to eliminate the words and text and instead limit the package description to images of cheerful babies and illustrations of contents. Unfortunately sales did not do well, as potential buyers in these countries would not purchase products which were perceived by them as containing powdered babies.

A company wishing to advertise their prestigious products in the Middle East illustrated its promotion brochure with a photograph of the armless statue of the Venus de Milo. The promotional literature was withdrawn, just in time, because in some Middle Eastern countries a severed hand or arm denotes a punished thief.

The advertisement of another exporter to a middle eastern country showed an illustration of women who were, unbeknown to him, promiscuous and this nearly led him into the local law court for publishing obscene literature.

Pepsi, a well-known American soft drinks company launched their products in China under the slogan 'Come alive with the Pepsi generation', when the slogan was (literally) translated into Chinese it read: 'Pepsi brings your ancestors back to life'. When this American slogan was initially translated into German it read: 'Come out of the grave with Pepsi'.

Another soft drinks company had their brand name translated into Mandarin Chinese and while the translation was phonetically accurate it was subsequently found that its literal translation changed its meaning to 'a female horse fattened with wax'.

A street trader in Vietnam sold packs of tiny plastic animals which were labelled with the following warning for parents: 'Be careful of being eaten by small children.'

During a car test marketing campaign in Saudi Arabia the phrase 'unbridled power' was translated from the English text into Arabic and then printed to accompany a picture of galloping horses. This was understood by some potential local buyers to mean 'a horse you cannot stop' and by others 'a car without breaks'.

Several years ago a European food company made the mistake of promoting their spaghetti sauce in Japan with the promise that its flavour was genuine Italian — this was a meaningless appeal to many Japanese who could scarcely find Italy on a map.

A car manufacturer intended to use the name Caprino to launch a new sports coupé. Just prior to the launch day it was pointed out that this meant goat's dung in some of the languages of the more important Mediterranean markets. This resulted in the name being changed to Capri.

When the McDonald Corporation developed its operation in France, its Big Mac slogan was pronounced as *'Gros Mac'* by the French, which is a slang expression for a big pimp. The name was quickly abandoned.

Care should be taken with composing mottos and logos, which are sometimes known as the strapline. Electrolux, the Swedish manufacturer of vacuum cleaners used the slogan 'Nothing sucks like an Electrolux'. This was most effective in promoting its products in European markets. When they used the same slogan to launch their products in the United States, they were made aware that the word 'sucks' means 'is very bad'.

Sometimes a word has a very different meaning in two different languages. Silver Mist was the brand name given to a range of conservatories or domestic greenhouses, where plants are grown. In the English context the word 'mist' might imply something associated with weather or nature, or related to the country, however when advertising the product with the same words in Germany it immediately created the impression that they were trying to sell a new type of outdoor lavatory, since the German translation of the word 'mist' is dung or manure.

Historically, in their teachings, some of the Western religions have used the naked and semi-naked human form to illustrate subjects or themes, and in the Western world the use of the human form in advertising, is nowadays accepted as normal. Many other cultures however, consider public display of female thighs and cleavages and in particular semi-nakedness as blasphemous and insulting and its use for advertising purposes would be considered by them, not only inappropriate but visually offensive and therefore subject to censorship.

Whether sales brochures and mail order catalogues for promotional use in some countries can or cannot include particular illustrations and pictures needs to be carefully investigated, if they are to reach their target audience. Representation of the human form, or certain animals and birds may, for religious reasons, be disapproved of, as may for example wine or beer glasses for alcoholic beverages, representation of the Christian cross, pictures of the clergy, monks and nuns, or the Star of David.

Means and ways of advertising vary greatly between countries. Some permit all means and ways while others permit only a few. The medium used for advertising can include — newspapers and magazines, radio, television, the internet, telephones, mobile phones and other hand-held devices, posters, billboards, illuminated advertising on buildings and freestanding sites, sandwich boards (carried a person who walks the streets and displaying posters on a solid board carried on his back and/or front), inside and outside public and private transport vehicles such as trains, buses and taxis, river and sea-going vessels, aircraft, airships and balloons; mobile advertising vans; mobile loudspeaker vans and sky-writing. It also includes advertising in cinemas using films and cartoons. Video films including those for private viewing sometimes also carry advertising material.

Even in those countries where on various political or religious grounds all forms of advertising is subject to censorship, such censorship is seldom 100% effective as commercial information and political ideas can cross physical borders by means of radio and television.

Also read

- Information, operating instructions and methods of use
- Interpreting and translating
- Signs, pictorial representations, emoticons and other symbols

Aesthetics or Appreciation of Beauty

Aesthetics relates our senses and our responses to objects. Taste, for example — sourness and intensity; smell, for example — sweetness and strength; sound, for example — pitch and melody; vision, for example — shape and colour; touch, for example — smoothness of an object or its shape, are all elements of aesthetics. While it may not have a major impact on economic activity, nevertheless it is relevant not only to the arts, music, drama and dance, but it also applies to accepted views on wearing clothing appropriate to the occasion or situation, how food is arranged and presented at a meal, to floral arrangements, to other forms of ornamentation as well as the design, colour and brand name of products.

There are not only regional differences concerning aesthetics for example dissimilarities between those living in Western Europe as opposed to those living in Eastern Europe, and between Europe and Asia, but also quite noticeable differences between those living in different countries.

The appreciation and significance of colours varies from culture to culture. Colours and colour combinations are usually judged by aesthetic standards and what may appeal to many people in Finland may appear ugly or unpleasant to those in Spain. Tableware designed and decorated for the British market may have no aesthetic appeal to buyers in Egypt and vice-versa. Car manufacturers have found that in some countries a metallic paint finish has greater aesthetic appeal than cars finished in solid colours.

Even when designing jackets or covers for books to be sold in two different English-speaking markets, for example in the United Kingdom and in the United States, it is necessary to take account of differences in national aesthetic appreciation. The publisher of a crime fiction book for the British market decided that the book jacket required softer pigments and more representational design, whereas the American edition required bolder colours and a more abstract design.

Music used for advertising messages or promotions needs to take into account its effect on the listener. An aboriginal assimilates his musical culture as part of his existence, a Western student may have *learned* to understand a Beethoven symphony. It is often suggested that any company intending to use music in its operation should 'go native' and adapt local music. Increasingly however, modern forms of communications such as the radio, television, films, CDs, DVDs and the internet, are reducing and obscuring these differences.

The design of buildings, equipment, products and packaging should be sensitive to local aesthetic preferences. This may sometimes pose problems with a company's wish for international uniformity.

Aesthetic standards also include the concept of symmetry. In the United Kingdom, for example, there is a distinct preference for symmetry in the household decor and if there is a chair on one side of a fireplace there is usually one on the other side, perhaps with a sofa in between. In the Netherlands people prefer a good composition but do not feel a need for symmetry.

The positioning of items of furniture and fittings in a room are considered to be more important in some cultures than in others. In a number of South Eastern Asian countries, including Hong Kong and Singapore considerable emphasis is placed on the ancient Chinese concept of aesthetics — Feng Shui. This refers to the relationship between nature and ourselves, so that we might live in harmony within our environment. If a mirror should hang in an inauspicious position, for example in relation to a window, this might well be considered unlucky to say the least, particularly if no action was taken to move it to a more auspicious or appropriate position. It might influence which way a doorway should face, where a bathroom should be installed and which position and direction a bed should be placed. Detractors of Feng Shui claim, tongue in cheek, that it has become a form of architectural acupuncture.

Cultural factors determine a society's perception of the human body and beauty. There are societies where it is believed that plumpness in men and women is synonymous with contentment, just as there are other societies where the opposite view prevails. Such views and perceptions are not as static as they were in the past and in some countries, the younger and better educated are increasingly influenced by current medical views about health and diet.

Aesthetics as well as language and legislation effect the choice of brand names. Sometimes the best brand name is a word in the local language and one which pleases local preference. Some trans-national and international companies select names or words that are pronounceable in most commercially useful languages and at the same time may not have any specific or adverse implications.

Also read

- Colour preferences and prejudices
- Food, drink and eating lifestyle
- Ergonomics and product design
- Taboos, superstitions and non-religious beliefs
- The way of life, lifestyle or quality of life

AGE

In many societies great respect is paid to age and this convention also applies to business-related activities, where age equals rank.

Often known as the seniority system, it is more frequently found in regions such as Asia and South East Asia than in Western culture countries. In Singapore for example, in the more traditional Chinese companies, hierarchy is often based on age, the oldest person having the greatest input, while in more modern trans-national companies hierarchy may well be based on ability and achievement.

It is always worthwhile to ascertain before travelling to another country whether businesses are being directed by young or old persons. In some business cultures people rise through the ranks at a meteoric rate and the young are permitted to do business with their elders, this is not necessarily the same in all cultures. It might therefore be inappropriate to send out a 30 year old business person to a country where the other party would normally expect to deal with an older person, unless of course this had been made apparent in earlier correspondence.

Several Asian cultures and societies which include the Japanese, Korean, Chinese and Vietnamese are using a form of age calculation, known as East Asian age reckoning. A new born baby is considered as one year old at birth and at each following New Year, but not its birthday, one year is added its age. This is different from the Western age system where a baby, when, born is zero year old. One consequence of this system is that East Asian persons are usually one to two years older in their reckoning than they would be in Western age system countries. The East Asian age reckoning is mainly used by the older generations as well as for divinations, fortune-telling and obituaries. The younger generations in these cultures increasingly use the Western age system and celebrate Western culture birthdays.

One is reminded of the following delightful age-related story. A little girl was sitting on her grandfather's lap as he read her a bedtime story. From time to time she would take her eyes off the book and reach up to touch his wrinkled cheek. She was by turns stroking her own cheek and then his again. Finally, she spoke up, 'Grandpa, did God make you?'

'Yes, darling,' he answered, 'God made me a long time ago.'

'Grandpa, did God make me too?'

'Yes, indeed, darling,' he said, 'God made you just a little while ago'. Feeling their respective faces again, she observed, 'God's getting better at it, isn't he?'

Also read

- Business ideology, management style and decision making

ALCOHOL

Although the consumption of alcohol is forbidden by some religions, it should however be noted that within every faith or religion there are those who strictly observe their beliefs, while there are others who treat them more casually. Many religions permit or tolerate consumption of alcohol, except during particular religious festivals.

In a few of those countries where consumption of alcohol is forbidden on religious grounds, foreign visitors may be able to obtain drinks in major hotels and restaurants. It might however be unwise to offer alcoholic beverages to one's host or one's guest, and therefore non-alcoholic drinks should be made available.

There are prepared foods including soups, main courses and desserts that are prepared with or contain alcohol. It is therefore important when entertaining visitors who, for religious, secular or medical reasons, abstain from consuming alcohol are not offered or served with such food.

A story was published in a British newspaper that that in the 1960's the British Foreign Minister had attended a formal dinner held in Peru where unfortunately he consumed too much alcohol. After the dinner and hearing music he is said to have asked a figure in a purple frock for a dance. The response had been, 'No,

First you are drunk. Second, this is not a waltz, it is the Peruvian national anthem. And third, I am not a woman, I am the Cardinal Archbishop of Lima.'

There are also countries, for example Saudi Arabia, where alcoholic beverages may not be imported nor consumed in any public place, for example in hotels, and any contravention of laws and regulations is subject to heavy penalties.

Rules and regulations concerning alcohol should be borne in mind when giving gifts to persons from countries where consumption of alcohol is forbidden for religious reasons. Inappropriate gifts would also include any food and confectionery containing alcohol.

One should also be aware that every country has its national drink and driving regulations in regard to maximum permitted blood alcohol level and its enforcement policies.

A manufacturer of a liqueur decided to call his product Scottish Mist. The product was well-made, had a pleasing flavour, and was marketed in an attractive bottle with a gold-coloured label. Unfortunately the product was not marketable in German-speaking countries, as the word 'mist', when translated into German, means dung or manure.

Also read

- Cars and driving
- Religious beliefs
- Smoking

ANIMALS, BIRDS AND PETS

In most of Western culture countries animals, particularly dogs and cats, are kept as pets rather than as working animals. The exceptions being dogs used for hunting, for guiding the blind, guard dogs and dogs used for anti-terrorist and rescue work. In Europe and North America dogs are considered man's best friend and in some countries, particularly France, dog owning has been elevated to that of a major status symbol.

There are however some Muslim countries where for religious and cultural reasons dogs are considered unclean animals and therefore do not enjoy any special status. In these countries there may be conventions which indicate that dogs must not be kept as pets, that dogs must not touch people, and that they cannot be used in advertisements.

One should be aware that there are some countries where to call a person a dog or a pig is a major insult. In Germany the expression *schweinhund* (pig-dog) is just about the strongest form of personal abuse. On the other hand there are other cultures where an animal-related term of familiarity or nickname is a term of affection.

In a country in the Far East, prior to a visit to the offices of the Senior Government Minister by a very important American political leader, a sniffer dog, that is a dog trained to detect explosives, was brought in to check the Minister's office for bombs. This almost caused a diplomatic incident since in that country's culture dogs were perceived as unclean animals and certainly not allowed inside offices or houses.

In Western culture countries the consumption of dog meat is generally considered taboo, in other countries for example China, Korea and Vietnam dogs, are a source of food and some breeds considered a culinary delicacy and used in the preparation of soup. In these countries it is claimed that it improves the stamina and virility of the consumer. A similar view is taken in Southern China and Northern Vietnam in regard to cats.

While in some countries horses are primarily bred and kept for sporting purposes such as hunting and racing, and for leisure activities such as riding and dressage, there are many other countries where they are primarily kept as working animals. Many

British animal lovers are horrified when they see that horsemeat is sold in butcher's shops in France as well as being on the menu in restaurants. One should be aware that the same revulsion is felt by Hindus and some other religious groups, when they see the meat of cows and calves, which are animals venerated by their castes and sects, in butchers' shops in Western culture countries.

Many religious groups and cultures consider the pig an unclean animal and pork and pork products may not be eaten by their members. There are many countries in the Middle East which do not permit the import of pork and pork products nor its consumption.

In some European countries, particularly Austria and Germany, the pig is considered to be a symbol of good fortune and used in many symbolic illustrations associated with the New Year. Floral arrangements and shop window displays are decorated with images of little pigs sometimes in combination with a chimney sweep. In the United Kingdom the pig is sometimes associated with thrift and saving and the name for a small money box in the shape of a small pig with a slot for coins is called a piggy bank.

In some countries it is an omen of bad luck if one sees a black cat crossing a road. In other countries a cat unexpectedly coming into a house is the sign of arrival of money. In India there is a cultural bias against cats and therefore very few people keep cats as pets.

Animosity between cats and dogs is assumed in some countries and people who cannot get along are said to have dog-and-cat relationships. In Japan however such an animosity is attributed between dogs and monkeys.

Languages differ in onomatopoeia — which are formations of a word by imitating the sound associated with an object or action. When, for instance advertising petfood, or using animals for promotional purposes which is in any case a culturally high risk approach, it is essential to realise that even in animal language there are cultural differences. In Japan a dog's bark is transliterated as wan-wan, in Italy bau-bau, in Spain guau-guau and in Norway vovvov. In Japan the sound made by cats is nyan-nyan or nyaw, while in the USA this is written as meow, as miaou in France and as ngeong in Indonesia.

The following is said to have occurred during a lesson in English as a second language where the teacher was revising the vocabulary of animal names. Each student was asked to give the name of an animal which had not been previously mentioned during the lesson. Unexpectedly one of the students said 'Lacoste'. This caused considerable puzzlement until the teacher finally realised that this name referred to the logo of a reptile on sportswear. The student was then asked whether he meant an alligator or a crocodile. He said that he thought that it was neither but another group of carnivorous reptiles. Needless to say the student was nicknamed Lacoste ever after.

In some countries and societies pictorial representations of animals, birds, spiders, snakes and fish may have specific religious or cultural connotations or associations. It is essential to be aware of these implications before using such images for advertising and marketing products or services.

Also read

- Taboos, superstitions and non-religious beliefs

APPOINTMENTS

In those countries where punctuality is considered a virtue and where the concept 'time is money' applies, it is essential to be punctual for appointments. In these countries the concept of punctuality is almost an obsession and profuse apologies may be called for if one arrives even five minutes late. There are also many other countries, for example in the Middle East, where a different and a much more casual attitude to time exists. Even in these countries visitors should make reasonable efforts to be punctual but be prepared to spend some time being kept waiting. Sometimes the waiting period may be due to the host being busy, but it could also be a coded message indicating lack of interest or the visitor's inferior status.

Cultural factors also apply in respect of how far ahead one requests an appointment. In many industrialised countries one or two weeks might be the minimum in others this may be too long and three or four days may be preferable. Requesting an appointment at the last minute could be interpreted as an insult by those persons who feel that one has not thought them sufficiently important to allow suitable lead time.

In some parts of the world broken appointments are not unusual, this is not necessarily a sign of rudeness or reluctance to do business, but simply that in some societies people have less respect for fixed appointments than those in Western industrialised countries. If, however, one wishes to transact business in a particular country or society it is essential that one conforms with their code of behaviour and conventions.

In other parts of the world, for example the Melanesian and the Arabian Gulf regions, the local concept of time can make it difficult to arrange appointments and to conduct business.

One should also be aware that there are some countries, such as Egypt, where different timekeeping conventions apply to foreign officials and business visitors as distinct from those applicable to local people. While foreign visitors would be expected to be punctual, an Egyptian government official or business executive could be late for a meeting.

It is also essential to be aware of local business hours before requesting an appointment. There are countries where appointments can seldom be arranged before mid-morning or around 10.00 o'clock (10.00 h). Hours of business of government offices, banks and commerce and trade are determined by many factors including national and local days of rest; annual holidays; religious holidays and festivals, prayer times, meal times and seasonal differences in working hours. Where people start work early, it may well be possible to arrange an early morning appointment. In some parts of the United States it is not unusual to make an appointment for a 'working breakfast', a formula which combines business with a meal. There are other countries where this concept would be considered most uncivilised.

Also read

- Business meetings
- Measuring and managing time
- Punctuality, duration and terminating a business visit
- Sense of time

ATTITUDES

Some societies are socially more tolerant than others. This can, for instance, apply to the concept of time and how people relate to one another. One example of this is the kind of service people expect in a retail food shop as distinct from a self-service type of grocery outlet. When it is their turn to be served at the counter Northern Europeans or Americans, for example, would expect the shop assistant to attend to all their requirements before attending to the next person. In other cultures, for example in Italy, if a customer wanted to sample a slice of sausage before making a purchase, the shopkeeper having cut a slice of sausage for this customer might well ask others waiting to be served whether they too would also like to sample a piece, and if so, promptly offer them a slice, before finalising the first customer's order.

Another example is people meeting for the purpose of business. Northern Europeans and North Americans usually view their relationship as primarily one between business associates, which takes priority over any friendship that may eventually develop. If therefore a deal is in the balance they tend to react unfavourably to any offer of gifts before a deal is signed, almost as if it signified sleaze or bribery, while on the other hand being happy to invite or being invited by the other party to a dinner afterwards. In other societies the process works the other way round. Their view being that since it may be unreliable to do business with strangers, a more appropriate way is to establish a bond of friendship through some form of hospitality before getting down to any business discussions.

There are some cultures and societies where people are basically optimistic. They do not like communicating bad news and will therefore always say what they think the other person would like to hear. One hears of the expression 'bad news never travels upwards'. This could have serious consequences if one is not aware of this attribute and if the information received is taken at its face value. If one suspects something is wrong, it is better to ask a direct question and find out how, in that society, bad or disagreeable news is transmitted. It may be that it is only obtained through a private and trusted advisor and it may well be that it is almost always better done in private.

While generalisations about people and countries contain more than a grain of truth, business executives often make a mistake in assuming that all those living in a particular Continent or Region are very similar. This assumption is often wrong. Taking Asia for example, a Japanese person tends to be more formal while a Korean is more informal and outgoing. Those of Arabic culture and living in Morocco, Yemen, Saudi Arabia and Syria differ greatly in their attitudes and conventions. In Scandinavia there are striking differences between persons from Finland and those from Norway, similarly within the European Union between say, a Greek and a person from Ireland.

It often takes considerable knowledge and insight into a foreign culture to distinguish between what rings true and is true, and what rings true but is not. In Italy for example, a person of integrity may well call upon the Deity to act as their witness and this is often done, without necessarily any intention to deceive. In the United

Kingdom however, as soon as one hears the expression 'May God strike me dead' uttered as proof of honesty, one is usually put on one's guard.

Also read

- Bribery and corruption
- Business entertaining
- Ethnic stereotypes
- Giving and receiving gifts
- Measuring and managing time

BODY LANGUAGE AND NON-VERBAL COMMUNICATION

Some scientists have suggested that of the total impact of a message 7% is verbal, 38% is vocal, that is tone of voice, inflection and other sounds and 55% is non-verbal.

Communication equipment for body language includes the eyes, the mouth, the hands, as well as body posture and movement. Only some of the many different postures, movements and gestures may be used or practised in a particular country or society and therefore many are unknown, this includes winking and the gesture of briefly raising and dropping of shoulders (shrugging).

Natural observers of people for example restaurant waiters and street traders, can often tell the nationality of persons just by observing non-verbal clues. It is stated that women are usually more perceptive than men, which is thought to be the result of mothers communicating with their babies solely on a non-verbal level during the early months of their life.

Facial expression can indicate attitude to others. Sayings such as 'his face is like an open book', or 'it was written all over his face', can usually apply to persons from one's own society or culture but might lead to misunderstandings when observing those from others.

When observing what appears to be a smile because the corners of the mouth are turned up it is not necessarily a sign of happiness and a more accurate indication whether a person is smiling would be the creases in the corners of the eyes. Nor when people smile does it always mean that they are pleased or amused. In Thailand it is also an expression for repairing minor breaches of etiquette, or to hide embarrassment, or to thank someone for a small service in which case it might be accompanied by a slight nod of the head.

Misunderstandings can arise in many ways; a strong expression of emotion by one person may appear as hostility to another, when in fact it might only be an expression of confusion. Often incorrect conclusions are reached unconsciously since they are based on our observation of body movements of persons in our culture. When observing people from other societies whose movements are different from ours, it often results in comments, such as lazy, indifferent, or even arrogant, which may not be accurate because it is quite simply due to their body language being different from ours.

In many countries shaking the head from side to side indicates no or negation, while nodding the head up and down indicates yes or assent. Problems arise in those cultures where these signals mean precisely the opposite as, for example, in Sri Lanka and several other Asian countries.

Eye contact including the length, intensity and direction of gaze, both when talking and listening, differs from culture to culture and is a common cause of misunderstanding. In some countries in Europe, to be able to look the person with whom one is doing business, straight in the eye, is often interpreted as a sign of trustworthiness, but in Thailand one would be better advised to deflect one's eyes, as staring at a person would be considered not only extremely rude but also an insult signal. A Swedish manager in Saudi Arabia considered the Pakistanis working for him to be insolent because when he criticised them for their slow work they refused to look him in the eye. He was unaware that they were in fact showing him a sign of respect, because their culture it is disrespectful to look one's superior or elder in the eye.

Touching a person is very much a part of body language. In Western culture for example, people like to touch those they are fond of. Shaking the hand of a man or woman on meeting and leaving is normal practice in some countries, but would be most inappropriate in those countries, for instance in India or in Thailand, where for a man to touch a woman, even if only her hand, is taboo and where the appropriate gesture is to place the palm of the hands together and bow slightly. Similarly, while in many Western countries children are often patted on the head as a gesture of friendship, this would be a most offensive gesture in those countries, particularly in Thailand, where the head is considered to be sacred and the holiest part of the body. In those countries where traditionally ablutions were, and often still are, performed with one's left hand, another person should not be touched with that hand. Even if leaning over another person's shoulder at a business meeting or when handing something over or receiving anything, the right hand should generally be used. In some countries there may be formal occasions when it is considered polite to use both hands, for example in China and Japan, when presenting one's business card.

In many of the Middle Eastern countries and also in some countries of South East Asia, it is considered extremely impolite to sit in such a way that the sole of one's shoes or feet are pointing at a person and one should therefore avoid sitting in such a particular attitude. There are also some countries like Japan where it is more polite not to sit with one's legs crossed.

The space or spatial zones around persons are also culture related. Just as there are animals who mark their territorial boundary by defecating around them, so people have their own 'space bubbles' or zones. The size of a person's special zone or territory is dependent on many factors including the country of birth and/or residence, population density of the country, and who is being admitted into it. The zone for a member of the family and other intimates is usually closer or smaller than the one for friends, and one would normally stand much further away from complete strangers. The problem arises when people from countries with different perception of the dimension of their personal spatial zones, meet. The one may move forward to stand at his culture's acceptable distance, while the other moves back to a distance which he considers more comfortable. During this period of forward and backward movements, each may well put an incorrect interpretation on the other person's physical movements. To be aware of the appropriate distance or personal space in a given culture is even more important when one party is male and the other female.

Other aspects of personal space include the way people position themselves when talking to one another. In some cultures persons appear to have more difficulty in communicating not only if they are not facing each other, but if they are not face-to-face in quite close proximity.

Olfaction, the sense or process of smelling, is yet another form of communication and attitudes towards smells, be they perfume, body odour or breath, are very much culture related. While in some societies it may be permissible to openly discuss perfume and perfumed hair lotion, but to talk about sexual, body or foot odour may be taboo.

To someone from Asia a person from Europe or North America may smell different, possibly because of the amount of meat they consume. Certain smells, the smell of baking for example, bring back pleasant memories. Then there are foreign smells, for example the smell of garlic is often unpleasant to those who live in countries where it is uncommon to eat it, while those who come from garlic eating cultures might not even notice the smell. Some people spray their offices with various synthetic perfumes or fresheners to replace so-called bad smells with more desirable fragrances, but to others these sprays smell unpleasant.

People in some cultures consistently breathe on one another when they talk, because to smell one's friend is not only nice but desirable, and to deny the other person your breath is to act ashamed. In other cultures the convention is exactly the opposite and people are trained not to breathe in other people's faces.

When therefore people from different cultures and conventions meet they may by their involuntary movements or expressions communicate signals which can result in misunderstandings.

Also read

- Conversation and communication
- Forms of address and use of titles
- Gestures
- Greeting, introductions, modes of address and leave-taking
- Perception of space

BRIBERY AND CORRUPTION

The following paragraph was published a few years ago in a European Community magazine: *'Corruption — the misuse of public power for private profit, has probably existed for as long as there has been public power. To eliminate corrupt officials and avaricious businessmen it would probably be necessary to change human nature.'*

Many of those familiar with international trade and commerce would agree with the often heard statement 'bribery is not condoned anywhere in the world, even in countries where it is a general practice.' A wide range of different words and expressions are used to cover bribes and bribery. In some countries it is not only customary but part of the culture and of social customs and practices and not in any way considered different from giving a tip for special services provided, except that in the case of bribes, such payments are usually expected to be made in advance.

One hears of gift culture, the principle of fair exchange in order to obtain a service or build up a co-operative relationship; the different importance attached to written documents in certain cultures, the co-existence of written and unwritten laws — corrupt practices fall under the latter heading. However corrupt practices are certainly not part of a cultural heritage and it would be more accurate to state that such practices are usually legitimised only by those who derive a benefit from the system of corruption.

This is just one of those instances where it is essential to know the local rules or to seek local advice, since in some countries one would most certainly be committing an offence, perhaps even finishing-up in prison, while in others one would be wasting one's time even visiting the country if one did not act in accordance with their time-honoured local customs and practices.

Even in Western culture countries which claim to have eliminated bribery one hears of very ingenious methods used to avoid or even evade legal restrictions which include providing hospitality, granting of low-interest loans, the 'loan' of real estate, purchase of otherwise unsaleable books or inflated fees for visiting lecturers.

Possibly the most appropriate piece of advice is the English proverb 'When thou art at Rome, do as they do at Rome'.

Bribes are sometimes disguised by euphemisms such as 'contribution', but still required to be paid in the same way as Al Capone (the famous 20th Century American gangster) called for charity handouts in Chicago. Other terms used include: facilitation payment, overdoers, compensation, speed money, tea money, and commission. In German it is called *Schmiergeld* – grease money, in France, *pot-de-vin* – a jug of wine, and the Italians call it *bustarella* – a little envelope.

It is also interesting to put this matter into an historical context. In Nigeria, the practice of 'dash' or a facilitation fee can be traced back to the 15th Century contacts with the Portuguese, when Africans solicited gifts or traded goods in exchange for labour.

Some multi-national British and American companies have admitted making facilitation payments in developing countries on the understanding that such payments were *tolerated*, not encouraged. They claim that under International Law such payments are not always illegal, although companies should clearly identify them in their accounts.

While in many countries the acts of giving and taking of bribes may well officially be illegal and frowned upon, in others it is an essential practice to pay-up, in order not to become caught up in an endless spiral of irritation and thereby enabling one to cut through frustrating bureaucracy. It must also be borne in mind that a business executive or official is not visiting a country to solve a philosophical or social problem, but is there to negotiate a contract or for some other specific reason.

The problems can perhaps be best illustrated by the following story. A person from North America bemoaned the incidence of corruption in the Indian Sub-Continent to his local joint-venture partner, who explained to him the continuity of this form of gift-giving with traditional exchanges with their priests. When the North American remained unimpressed the local partner added, here we give gifts after a law has been passed and you call it corruption, in your country you give gifts before the law has been passed and you call it lobbying.

When, some years ago, a negotiator visiting a country in South America resolved not to give 'inducements' under any circumstances it led him to a strict, even puritanical, neglect of giving tokens of his esteem, such as gifts. As a result he was locally regarded as discourteous. The locals considered the absence of appropriate tokens of esteem an insult, and one that implied that he simply had no power to confer or withhold a favour. He was ignored and had to return home since no-one was prepared to meet and do business with him.

Since the early 1990s the international community began to recognise corruption as a major obstacle to development, thereby hindering trade and investment. As a result of this an organisation, Transparency International, was launched in 1993 with the aim of exposing and curbing corruption.

In a report on Ethical practices and how to avoid corruption published in the United Kingdom it was recommended that businesses should create a register of all gifts and hospitality given, and that all customers be made aware of the company's policy regarding gifts before contracts are signed. The report acknowledged that it may not be possible to eliminate such payments immediately in some countries and it suggested that the means be developed to eliminate them completely over time.

In another United Kingdom press report it was stated that it is the practice for senior civil servants responsible for government contracts to accept hospitality from firms carrying out work for the government. In the United Kingdom senior civil servants are permitted to accept hospitality on condition that details are recorded into an official register. The comment was made that while there was no direct link between contacts awarded and hospitality accepted, many observers are concerned that close relationships can distort judgements.

The following is a true-life incident to illustrate this subject: at the end of a business trip to an East African country I made my way to the airport departure lounge via the customs desks. These were the days before electronic scanning machines, and luggage checking, if at all, was manual. Like all other travellers I was directed into a small room where the customs officer asked a few questions. He asked me if I had a wallet and followed this up by asking to let him see its contents. He then enquired if I really needed all the money I was carrying. My response, based on previously received advice from travellers to that country, was to take out some notes and give them to him. Nothing further was said and I was allowed to proceed, board the plane and fly home. To this day I have not made up my mind whether this was pure extortion or an exit facilitation payment.

Also read

- Giving and receiving gifts
- Tipping and gratuities

BUSINESS CARDS

It may be obvious but it is important that one's own name is shown on one's business card. Also shown on the card should be one's title, professional or business title or occupation as well as the name of the organisation or company one represents.

Business cards to be used in countries where the Arabic script and alphabet is used should be printed in that language. Similarly when visiting China where they must be printed in Chinese characters and those to be used in Japan must be printed in the appropriate Japanese characters and script. In those countries with languages into which one's name cannot be literally translated, for example languages such as Arabic, Chinese, Japanese, Korean and Russian a transliteration of one's name may well be required. Where the written characters used are different from that used in one's own country, it is customary to have one side of the business cards printed in one's own language and on the reverse side in the language of the country one is visiting.

Great care should be taken with the style and content of business cards and in particular whether professional and academic qualifications, honorific's and post-nominal's should be included. In Australia, for example, one's first name should be printed on business cards, as they consider an initial or just Mr. to be pompous.

On the business cards which I took to China my English name had been transliterated into 'Comfortable Horse', which did not cause me difficulties. Before my wife accompanied me on my next visit I ordered business cards for her from the same dependable supplier. Subsequently, during a meeting in China with a Chinese businesswoman my wife commented on the transliteration of my name and said she was curious how her name had been transliterated. The Chinese lady seemed a little discomfited when asked, but when gently persuaded suggested that it was a very fine name for a man. Naturally this increased our level of curiosity.

Eventually she let us know that it transliterated into 'a solid pile of stones'. Although afterwards a new translator-printer was found, this story indicates that before business cards are printed, a back translation of the name from Chinese into the original language, by another translator, is to be recommended.

In practically every country business or visiting cards are not only customary but essential, but in some regions, particularly in East Asia, there is what could be called, a business card etiquette, which indicates how cards should be presented and received. This etiquette recommends the degree of formality and style to be used. One should, for example, not just glance at it but read it with care and should receive it with some indication that it is of value. It should not, obviously, be deposited in a casual or nonchalant manner into one's pocket or briefcase.

In some countries it is the practice to present a card to each person to whom one is being introduced on the first business visit, in others cards are only exchanged between senior persons. There may be a further exchange of cards on subsequent visits.

In the United Kingdom, recipients of national honours are entitled to put the initials, without any punctuation between the individual letters, of the honour conferred on them on their business cards. These initials are printed immediately following their family name. There is the story about a British person giving his business card to a businessman from Andorra. In this case the British person was Mr Michael Smith, OBE. The Andorran looked at the card and Mr Smith was somewhat surprised to be addressed as Mr Obe.

Also read

- Forms of address and use of titles
- Greeting, introductions, modes of address and leave-taking
- Names
- Status symbols

Business Correspondence

It is preferable, at least for the initial correspondence with a business or person in another country, to be in the language of the recipient. It might subsequently be conducted in any other mutually acceptable language. This applies to all forms of communication be they letters, email, cables, telegrams, telex, facsimile, or other forms of transmission. If possible idiomatic expressions and colloquialisms should be avoided.

When writing in a well-known international language to a person in another country where a different language is used, it would still be courteous to include either a formal or a non-formal translation of the letter.

There are various conventions regarding the way in which the date is written in correspondence, some use the day/month/year system, others, for example in the United States, month/day/year, and sometimes in Sweden, for example year/month/day. The convention used in Spain includes placing a full stop or period sign between the 1st and 2nd figure, for example 2.009.

Trade literature and catalogues which may be multilingual in presentation should, whenever possible, include an introduction or a covering letter in the language of the recipient. When trade literature and catalogues are targeted at countries where languages are written and read from right to left this or as usually is the case in Japan, China and Korea vertically from top to bottom and then ordered from right to left, this should be, whenever possible and practical, be taken into account during their preparation.

One should be aware that in some countries it is a well established custom to leave unsolicited correspondence unanswered, even when it is in the local language, unless there is an active interest in the subject.

Particular care should be taken with the spelling of the title, name and business title of the person to whom one is writing.

In many countries the postal addresses of government offices, businesses and persons is only represented by a box number and gives no indication of their geographical location. Should it subsequently be decided to pay a visit, steps should be taken, before arriving in the country to establish their location and how to get there.

Conventions regarding signing a letter vary not only between companies but also from country to country. In some businesses letters are signed but it is their policy not to give any indication of the name and position of the signatory or signatories. In others both name and appointment appear below the signature. In some countries it is customary for official and business letters to be signed by more than one person, one being a manager with restricted authority and the other an executive with full authority.

The custom of using abbreviations or leaving out letters to make a word shorter is practised in many languages, and while they may well be understood by those writing in their mother tongue it could lead to misunderstanding when writing to those who conduct their affairs in other languages. Examples of this are English language abbreviations i.e. or ie = that is; e.g. or eg = for example; and lbs = pounds. This could be a problem if the abbreviation had a different meaning in another language, for example the abbreviation Nr or No can be used instead of number or near.

Except for some of the internationally well know acronyms such as UN which stands for United Nations, many of the other acronyms as used in one's own language may not be understood in other languages.

Conventions and appropriate nuances regarding opening and closing salutations for correspondence vary from country to country. In some English speaking countries the appropriate form of closing salutation may be the informal 'Yours sincerely', the semiformal 'Yours truly', or the more formal 'Yours faithfully'. When writing in the French language it would be appropriate to close a letter with a form of words traditionally used in France, which requests the recipient 'to accept the assurance of my most distinguished sentiments' — *'Nous vous prions d'agréer, M/Mme, l'expression de nos sentiments les plas dévoués'.*

In the United Kingdom there is a convention to personalise a letter when, for example, addressing a senior government official or politician, or a business colleague, and in these cases to 'top and tail' the letter, and the words 'Dear Mr X' and 'Yours sincerely' are hand-written and not typed. In other countries where this is not a normal practice, this custom may however be thought to be unusual, if not in bad taste.

Also read

- Greeting cards
- Interpreting and translating
- Names

BUSINESS ENTERTAINING

Sharing food has always been a fundamental expression of friendship. The host honours his guest by putting his needs above all else and the guest, through his behaviour strives to show himself worthy of such honour. Entertaining of a guest might take the form of a meal around midday in some countries, in others it takes place in the evening. Official banquets are in some countries the only form of social contact between persons in a business or governmental relationship, particularly where casual or informal entertaining does not exist.

Whether a guest should or should not be invited to a night club, a casino or other places of entertainment is not only culture related, but also dependent on the religious beliefs and observance of such beliefs on the part of one's guest.

Eating habits and customs vary not only from country to country, but also within countries by regions and local traditions in respect of meal occasions, meal times, seating arrangements, type of food served at different meals and the way food and beverages are served and eaten, forms of entertainment during or after a meal and when to leave.

Other culture related issues are, how we eat. In between taking a bite or drink, should one put one's hand, wrist, elbows or forearms on the table or keep one's hands in one's lap? In German-speaking countries of Europe young adults are cautioned, usually early in their life not to put their hands in their lap, as it could suggest that some form of sexual action might be going on under their napkin or serviette. Since people in different countries and societies have a wide range of table manners and conventions the only practical advice is – *watch your host or hostess.*

While in some societies is it not only customary but complimentary to eat with obvious enjoyment and in an audible fashion, be it a belch or smacking one's lips, in others this would be considered most impolite.

In some countries it is customary for a guest who has been invited to a meal, be it in a restaurant or in a private house, to send flowers to the hostess either before or afterwards, in others it is customary to bring flowers, chocolates or other appropriate gifts.

Ways of attracting the attention of a waiter or waitress in restaurants are highly culture-oriented and what might be considered a perfectly normal gesture or signal in one country could well be construed as highly offensive in another. The range of signals include verbal hissing sounds or 'psst-psst', or an exclamation of 'Herr Ober' (Mr Waiter) in the German language, or 'Waiter' in England. While gestures such as snapping of fingers or clapping might be quite acceptable in some societies, they are not in others. In Thailand one would beckon the waiter with the right palm down, moving the finger rapidly towards oneself.

There is the story of an Englishman having a meal with a Danish executive who asked him if he liked 'earrings'. He replied that he thought that they looked nice on a lady but that he himself would not wear them. When the Dane looked puzzled they talked this through and then found out that in Danish the word 'herrings' is spoken to sound like 'earrings'. One should bear this tale in mind and be aware that there is often a significant difference between the written and spoken word. Those whose mother tongue is English are often amazed how their spoken language becomes incomprehensible when spoken by foreigners. Non-English speakers have the same experience when British persons try to speak in their language. In all languages dialects and accents can cause misunderstandings because of mispronounced words.

Also read

- Alcohol
- Flowers and giving of flowers
- Food, drink and eating lifestyle
- Gestures
- Giving and receiving gifts
- Language
- Religious beliefs
- Social contact
- Table etiquette and eating
- Women in business and the professions

BUSINESS IDEOLOGY, MANAGEMENT STYLE AND DECISION MAKING

Ideology is defined as any system of belief publicly expressed with the clear purpose of influencing the sentiments and actions of others. It includes attitudes to profit, business structures, decision making, negotiating practices and business morality.

International managers and those negotiating on an international level are as a rule aware that there are often considerable national and cultural differences in business ideology, organisation structure, education and social stratification, in companies throughout the world when comparing, for example, those operating in Western culture countries with Japan, or those in the Indian subcontinent with those in South America or the Middle East.

In small businesses it is usually the owner, or the family or perhaps a manager who make the decisions. In larger organisations tradition and culture often determines the decision-making process. The three predominant processes or systems include the consensus or committee basis, the centralised and the decentralised systems.

There are differences in the way people engaged in business interact and communicate. In some countries and societies there is a high rate of verbal interaction, in others it is low and this is counterbalanced by higher volume of written communication. In American organisations, for example, face-to-face interaction is usually higher than in French ones. The reasons for these differences are usually culture based. French organisation culture has been influenced by and derived from the Catholic Church, the army and government, while in the United States it is the other way round, and it is business organisations that have influenced the church, the army and governmental organisation.

In many countries in Asia, business is often a personal affair and almost everything, be it products or profit, take second place. In these countries it is therefore essential to establish good personal relations with a large network of people. It may be thought that with the right product and right price one can do business. This is not always the case and it may be necessary to approach a company in the 'correct manner' through acceptable introductions and at the appropriate management level. This level may be the company president, or chief executive officer, but on the other hand it may not, if for example, managers further down the line of command are the real decision-makers. Culture related factors have a bearing on the decision making process, up to and including an agreement or contract.

There is the famous management style tale of an American oil rig supervisor in Indonesia who yelled at one of his employees to take a boat to the on-shore dock. In an Indonesian culture context it is not done to tell off or shout at a person in public, and as a result of this terrible faux pas the supervisor was chased by a mob of outraged workers carrying hatchets and axes.

In Japan consensus in decision making is the style used by the great majority of the firms irrespective whether they are small, medium or large. Although this form of decision making may be slow when judged from a Western culture perspective, but once made, implementation is generally smooth and effective. This is therefore different from the method used by firms in most Western culture countries where decisions are often taken more quickly whilst their implementation is slower than under the Japanese system.

Once a decision has been taken and an agreement is reached, further culture related factors come into play. In some Western culture countries the attitude is usually that contracts should be honoured as initially stated, while to the Japanese, for instance, once an agreement has been reached it is not unethical, but probably most rational to consider changes that may lead to a more desirable agreement, especially if there are any changes in circumstances.

The basic concept of a contract is not necessarily the same in all cultures and countries. Generally speaking, the Western world attaches much importance to a written contract, which is a statement of the obligations and considerations of the contracting parties. It is employed as a basis for minimising misunderstandings and enforcing compliance. When a contract has been signed, relationships proceed on a mutually acceptable solid basis. However in some countries a written contract is viewed more as an expression of intent at the time the agreement is made. It is signed to get the relationship started officially, thereafter everything is subject to change and negotiation. Under these circumstances a regard for personal relationships and mutual benefits are the foundation of any business arrangement and a contract is in essence nothing more than a symbol of this relationship.

Although it is often both dangerous and misleading to stereotype inhabitants of a country, or for that matter, any large set of persons belonging to a particular nation, there is nevertheless some element of fact in these generalisations, and this can provide a basis for general understanding. North Americans, for example, can be identified as individualists, southern Europeans as elitists and rank conscious, Japanese as consensus oriented and committed to their group. In many cases this means that business executives and government officials are unable to shake off the traditional habits and customs of their people.

In some of the countries in the African, Asian and Pacific regions which are sometimes known as part of the Pan-Islamic world, Islamic banking rules are more strictly enforced than in others. To pay, demand or accept interest is an offence under the Sharia principle of finance. This is an entirely different finance concept from that practiced in non-Islamic countries where interest underpins nearly all financial products. Never-the-less in some Islamic countries and in many secular countries with a Muslim majority, ways and means have been devised where standard Western style banking procedures and systems are operated or are operated on a parallel basis.

It should be noted that the Western concept of insurance, especially life insurance, may also may be disapproved of by some of those who interpret Islamic precepts in a more orthodox manner. The basic concept of insurance does however exist in the Pan-Islamic world in other formats.

Also read

- Age
- Intra-national and intra-regional differences
- Laws and legal systems
- Losing face and saving face
- Negotiating and bargaining
- Religious beliefs

Business Meetings

In many, if not most non-Western culture countries, it is considered impolite to start talking business immediately after being invited into someone's office. Sometimes considerable time will be spent exchanging pleasantries during which coffee or tea or other refreshments may be served which it would be most impolite to refuse. In a few of these countries it may only be later or perhaps even during the formalities of farewell that the visitor may discreetly mention the reason for his visit, which may then lead to a further invitation and visits.

In some Middle Eastern countries it is unlikely that a meeting with the person with whom one wishes to do business will be in private. There may be a dozen other people who might be present or ushered in to chat, sip coffee and pay their respects. This conference-style visit usage is an established way of doing business. It is quite usual and an accepted practice for other persons to walk in unannounced and interrupt. In due course one might be able to conduct meetings away from the office of the person with whom one wishes to do business, but this is unlikely to be the case at the first meeting.

On the other hand in Western culture countries, in particular in Europe and North America where the concept of 'time is money' applies, small talk before moving on to business matters, is generally limited and brief.

In some countries, particularly in the United States it is an acknowledged practice to have a 'working breakfast', which combines business with a meal. There are however other countries where this concept might be considered most uncivilised. While 'business lunches' are an accepted part of the business scene in many Western culture countries, in some countries, for instance Turkey there is a preference for long meetings followed by a prolonged lunch. A more recent development in Western culture countries has been 'business tea' which is an opportunity for shorter business meetings.

Also read

- Appointments
- Body language and non-verbal communication
- Business cards

CARS AND DRIVING

Car owners' perceptions of their cars vary and many different factors contribute to the final choice but motor manufacturers suggest that if one were to generalise, the average German would buy it because of its strength and engineering input, a Swede for its security, a British person for its stability and social status, an Italian because it goes 'vroom vroom' and a French person for its style and beauty.

When a chauffeur driven car is provided for a businessman and his wife, it is not the practice in every country that the wife enters the car first, followed by her husband. There are some many countries predominantly in the Middle East where it is customary for the man to enter first followed by his wife, and similarly when leaving the car.

There will also be different local customs and etiquette regarding business executives when accompanied by their male or female secretary. It sometimes helps to work out the dilemma, if one bears in mind that the car could under these circumstances be regarded as an extension of one's office in that country.

If a chauffeur driven car is sent to meet and collect business executives and one is not certain as to their relative status and consequent car seating arrangements for the visitors, the situation could be resolved by the chauffeur (or whoever is meeting the executive) to ask 'Excuse me, have you any preference in seating?' or 'Where would you like to sit?' While this might be called 'passing the baby', it would devolve the decision making process to the visitors who, one would assume, would themselves know their own respective status and preferences. Similar protocol might be applied when using a limousine or taxi.

Many motoring and other organisations publish books and guides with information dealing with various aspects of driving in other countries. Unfortunately most of them do not include any information about hand and arm signals given by policemen, traffic wardens and other authorised persons, nor about hand and arm signals given by other road users. However these signals, like other body language and gestures, can easily be misunderstood, resulting sometimes in no more than puzzlement but occasionally in more serious consequences. Drivers should be aware that some hand signals which have a clearly established driving related meaning in one's own country, may well have a very different meanings to drivers and other road users in another country. They could even represent an insult signal which could lead to further unfortunate end results. In the Balearic island of Menorca a leaflet in English, issued by a car hire company gave the following advice: *'If you see a motorcyclist or cyclist raise his left hand in front of you, this usually means he is turning right. But take care as the rider may not be local, in which case he may turn left.'*

One should be aware that there may well be local customs concerning the right of way regarding other road users such as stray animals, load-carrying animals, animal-drawn vehicles, cyclists and pedestrians.

Driving safely means different things in different countries. In Sweden it means keeping your headlights on all the time. In Germany it means being in control at 220 kilometres per hour. In Italy, being safe is just sounding the car horn.

In some countries, for example Germany, pedestrians must not cross a road regulated by traffic lights, if the light is red. Disobeying may lead to a fine. In the United Kingdom such disregard, although not approved, is considered normal.

In some countries the flashing of car headlights at on-coming traffic can mean 'get out of my way' in others 'come-on — I will let you have the right of way'. In the United Kingdom flashed headlights are usually interpreted as an invitation to a driver coming from the opposite direction to proceed, whereas in Cyprus it is more commonly a signal of 'I'm coming through'. In Mexico an oncoming vehicle flashing its headlights is warning you to slow down or to pull over because you are approaching a narrow stretch of road. It is also the local custom that the first car to flash lights has the right of way while the other driver is expected to yield.

National laws and regulations regarding driving differ greatly. In many Scandinavian countries, for example, it is an offence to drive after drinking any alcoholic beverage. In some countries, for instance Saudi Arabia, women are not permitted to drive a car.

There are no International rules and regulations which could be used as a reference of what may or may not be done in the event of a motor accident. It is always advisable to obtain relevant information from the International Division of a national motoring organisation before driving, or hiring and driving a vehicle in a foreign country. In some countries, if one is involved in an accident, the local law enforcement agents or the police will automatically detain all the main parties concerned until all details have been established. In other countries they may take statements from the parties concerned, this takes for granted that one has means of verbal communication with the police or representative of the local law enforcement agency.

In many of the developing countries people should, at any rate according to published national Road Traffic Regulations, either drive on the right or the left, many however choose to drive along the middle of the road. In these countries the most essential piece of car equipment, is the horn. The horn is sounded to warn of approach, greet friends, move offending camels, donkeys, street vendors, rickshaws, pedestrians, children and other road users out of the way, allow another road user onto the road rarely, and just because they feel like it. They also use it to warn the poor unfortunate traffic policeman, strategically positioned at every junction because drivers are either colour-blind or don't understand the significance of a traffic light, that the driver has absolutely no intention of slowing down or stopping, mostly because they couldn't even if they wanted to. The general maintenance of the horn is prized above all else, including whether or not there is of water in the radiator, petrol, diesel or whether the vehicle still has the correct number of wheels.

Also read

- Alcohol
- Gestures
- Travelling

CENSORSHIP

Censorship is practised in a number of countries for a variety of different reasons. It usually targets sexual, political, racial and/or religious issues, as defined by an ever-growing and ever-shifting assortment of forbidden and prohibited issues. It may, for example, be in the interest of preserving public morals or in conformity with the ideals of State.

Censorship can be applied in a variety of ways and means including the requirement for foreign language films to have sub-titles in the national or local language.

The Middle Eastern production company which wanted to dub or provide the Walt Disney epic film *The Lion King* with a new soundtrack in Arabic discovered, that they had to change two words at the heart of the story, namely 'lion' and 'king'. To confer these names on animals would not only have caused a serious affront to several rulers in the region, but guarantee a ban on the film. The production company had to change these names or find synonyms, such as 'Ruler of the Forest' instead of 'Lion King'.

Censorship rules might apply to the printed media whether written or illustrated including newspapers, magazines, books and the Internet; the spoken media including radio, and sound tracks of television, cinema films, animated cartoons and stage plays; the visual media including films, videos and the Internet; also included could be gramophone records and tapes, trade catalogues and brochures, product labels, paintings and other works of art, and posters.

Prior to planning and creating any form of advertising and promotional material to be used in another country it is essential to establish whether any form of censorship exists in the country concerned, and if so, its regulations must be taken into account.

The following anecdote circulated in the former Communist countries of Eastern Europe. A man dies and goes to hell. There he discovers that he has a choice: he can go to capitalist hell or to communist hell. Naturally, he wants to compare the two, so he goes over to capitalist hell. There outside the door is the devil, who looks a bit like President Ronald Reagan. 'What's it like in there?' asks the visitor.

'Well,' the devil replies, 'in capitalist hell, they flay you alive, then they boil you in oil and then they cut you up into small pieces with sharp knives.'

'That's terrible!' he gasps. 'I'm going to check out communist hell!' He goes over to communist hell, where he discovers a huge queue of people waiting to get in. He waits in line. Eventually he gets to the front and there at the door to communist hell is a little old man who looks a bit like Karl Marx. 'I'm still in the free world, Karl,' he says, 'and before I come in, I want to know what it's like in there.'

'In communist hell,' says Marx impatiently, 'they flay you alive, then they boil you in oil, and then they cut you up into small pieces with sharp knives.'

'But... but that's the same as capitalist hell!' protests the visitor, 'Why such a long queue?'

'Well,' sighs Marx, 'Sometimes we're out of oil, sometimes we don't have knives, sometimes no hot water...'

Also read

- Interpreting and translating
- Photography and other forms of visual recording
- Politics

CLASS SYSTEMS, CASTE AND SOCIAL STRUCTURE

A caste system is a form of class distinction usually based on birth, that is, it is hereditary. Where it has a strong religious base, it may determine the specific occupational and social roles of its members. The caste system is one of the elements of Hinduism. In some religions it is synonymous with the concept of the large joint family or the extended family, with its consequence of giving employment to members of the same, and often extended, family.

A class system, defined as a group of people of the same status, even in those countries where a society appears classless, there is usually a pecking order based on something other than class. It may be based on clan loyalties or dynastic connections, on social status, on wealth, on education, or perhaps being part of a network of good friendships.

This brings to mind the following story of an American college graduate who met an English lady on a trans-Atlantic liner en route to Europe. They had a wild affair ending with the seduction of the American boy. A little time later he attended a large and formal event in London and saw, among the other guests Lady A. He moved towards her and said: 'Hello, How have you been?' Lady A looked down her nose and replied

'I don't think we have been introduced' The young American was stunned and said,

'Surely you remember me' and then added 'Don't you remember that only last month we slept together?'

'And what' Lady A replied angrily, 'makes you think that constitutes an introduction?'

Difficulties do arise when someone visits another country and may not be aware or able to recognise the divisions and nuances of its hierarchical society, its class, title and rank structure. Often, as a foreigner in that country, one is automatically but unknowingly given an honorary status of the persons one is associated with. It is however most useful to find out about the local social pecking order so as to avoid misunderstanding and causing embarrassment.

Also read

- Education
- The family and the in-group
- The way of life, lifestyle or quality of life

Colour Preferences and Prejudices

Colour preferences and prejudices based on local, regional, national, religious, administrative or even political associations are to be found throughout the world. Often they are impossible to explain as their roots may lie in non-religious beliefs or folklore which are deeply rooted in the culture of the society and may be difficult or costly or even impossible to change. Awareness of colour preferences and prejudice is therefore important, particularly in marketing related activities as well as when giving presents.

In most Indo-European languages there are numerous highly differentiated terms for colours, there are, however, other languages which have a more limited range of terms.

Choosing an appropriate or suitable colour for a product and its packaging might well affect its performance in the market place, although short-lived fashion changes or crazes may occasionally override even ingrained views.

Trans-national car manufacturers know from experience that in addition to climatic factors that determine which colours and colour schemes are suitable for hot, for temperate and for cold climates, that people in many countries have national preferences and dislikes for particular colours. In some countries there are regulations while in others there are conventions regarding the colour of motor vehicles used for particular purposes. For example vehicles used by the post office, for public transport and for funerals.

The attitude to colour is self-evident in the language of some cultures, where people 'see red with anger', or when sad or depressed one might say to 'feel blue'. In the United Kingdom someone might feel 'green with envy', in Finland however the colour appropriate to envy is black.

Red is the most popular colour in China and is a Chinese symbol of good luck, happiness and festivity. On the other hand white is the colour for mourning whilst blue is associated with sorrow and a combination of these two colours should be avoided. Similarly in Japan a combination of black and white is reserved for funerals and should be avoided for wrapping of gifts.

While in the United Kingdom there is a tradition of blue for a boy and pink for a girl, in some parts of Belgium and in regions of Eastern France the implications of these colours are reversed.

The colour of garments worn on special occasions such as marriage, birth and death are very often different from those worn on other occasions. While in countries with a Western culture black signifies mourning, in some Far Eastern cultures the appropriate colour would be white. Likewise in Western cultures white would be the appropriate dress for weddings, while in some Eastern cultures it is red. In Singapore the colours red and pink are signs of joy and appropriately coloured paper would be used for invitations.

Even the colour of ink used for signing documents can have culture related consequences and in Korea signing a contract in red ink suggests that it will probably come to a bad end.

Colour also has a bearing on sales, as was found by an internationally well known oil company when marketing their products in a developing country. Their product range was traditionally marketed in their two colour company logo, but in spite of good promotional support, sales remained static. Eventually it was discovered that this particular two colour combination was considered unlucky. When the colour scheme was changed, sales increased dramatically.

One of the largest Spanish sugar confectionery company sells its products in Spain and other countries worldwide, in red and yellow coloured packs. When however selling in the fiercely nationalistic Basque region of Spain they found it necessary to change these colours to green and yellow or green and white. Likewise in Northern Ireland the colour combination of orange and green is to be avoided as it has divisive political connotations.

A company attempting to sell its beer in Hong Kong used a message that the beer was so good that even the Irish, who are great beer drinkers, liked it. The picture accompanying the advertisement showed an Irishman, who not surprisingly, as this was an advert created in Ireland, was wearing a green hat while drinking his beer. The sales promotion was not successful as the green hat is a traditional Chinese symbol used to identify a man as a cuckold.

Also read

- Flowers and giving of flowers
- Giving and receiving gifts
- Taboos, superstitions and non-religious beliefs

COMPLIMENTS

There are some societies, for instance in some parts of the Middle East, where it is not appropriate to express excessive admiration of one's host's belongings be they in his office or his home since, in conformity with local customs, one's host might feel obliged to make a present of the object concerned. This could apply to items such as a necktie, a cigarette lighter or else a house or garden plant, and therefore could cause considerable embarrassment to both parties.

In South America under similar circumstances social conventions advise that if after admiring an object in the home of a person it is offered as a gift, one should promptly find a suitable and elegant turn of phrase to decline such a present.

In Pakistan, as in most Western culture countries, it would be quite polite to compliment one's host on his home and possessions when invited into his house.

It is important to be aware that even paying compliments when greeting someone can be fraught with culture related complications. In some English speaking African communities, a person will greet another by saying, 'You have put on some weight.' While in the United States many people would be offended with this greeting, in Africa, it is a compliment that acknowledges how healthy and prosperous a person looks.

From a North American stand-point it would appear that giving compliments is more common in Western Europe than in the United States. In Western Europe for example, one can compliment someone on his language proficiency, particularly if it their second language.

Both in Western Europe and North America one should exercise caution if complimenting businesswomen or other female members of company staff about their looks or attire, unless they are personal friends, since this may not only be considered politically incorrect but could be misinterpreted as a form of sexual harassment.

Also read

- Giving and receiving gifts
- Social contact

Conversation and Communication

At business meetings it is customary in some countries particularly in the Middle East to indulge in innocuous or small talk before getting down to business. Such preliminary conversations might include topics such as cars, animals and pets, sport or by and large apolitical events about one's own country or the country one is visiting. One would normally avoid topics such as politics, religion and matters concerned with sex. In those countries where these conventions apply, this period of small talk serves to establish the integrity of the visitor, and vice-versa. There are, however, many other countries where such conduct on the part of either host or visitor would be considered as a waste of valuable executive time. It is therefore essential to ascertain customs and etiquette to ensure that one observes local practices.

Colloquialisms and slang terms can easily lead to misunderstandings and should therefore be used with care, if not avoided altogether.

Misunderstanding can arise during conversations when persons in some countries as for example in Korea, use the possessive 'our' instead of 'my', or the pronoun 'we' instead of 'I', particularly when they are speaking about themselves, their business or their home.

A wide range of customs and etiquette relating to conversation and general communication are observed in the various countires of the world, and it is therefore necessary to familiarise oneself with those in the country or one is visiting. In some of the Middle Eastern countries, it would be considered discourteous to ask about the health or wellbeing of someone's wife or daughters, instead one might quite in safety enquire after his family and sons.

What is perceived as loud in terms of volume of speech by persons from one culture may be considered as being quite normal or conventional by someone from another. Loudness of the voice varies from culture to culture ranging between a whispered conversation to a loud shout. This too can lead to misunderstandings where those who normally speak loud may interpret a low sound level conversation as conspiratorial, and conversely those who normally speak softly might consider that those speaking in a raised voice are aggressive.

Culturally determined behaviour reveals itself in many ways, even in communication. There is the story of a Russian lady travelling on a German airline. The pilot announced that the take-off would delayed by 2 hours due to bad weather at Frankfurt. A Russian lady called the hostess and then whispered to her 'Please, tell me the real reason!' The hostess drew herself up to her full height and said in a loud voice: 'Are you calling me a liar?' The point of this story is that Russians tend not to believe official announcements, and this lady was in fact showing how much she trusted the hostess on a personal level to tell her the truth.

Also read

- Body language and non-verbal communication
- Business Meetings
- Forms of address and use of titles
- Language
- Telephoning

COURTESY

Courtesy is more than just a polite or considerate act; it covers a wide range of actions including greetings, conversation and giving and receiving gifts, to mention a few. In many traditional societies it determines how people interact with one another, be it within their family, with their friends, with other in-groups and out-groups and with foreigners.

Words and expressions of gratitude such as 'please' and 'thank you' are not part of every language or culture. They are used more frequently in some cultures, where they form part of almost any request for service, than in others. Persons who are customarily used to such courtesies often perceive or interpret the non-use or absence of such expressions as rudeness on the part of the other person, because they fail to realise that it is very much a culture related convention. When someone from a Western culture country would say 'thank you', a person living in Indonesia for example, would probably smile or nod in acknowledgement. In Thailand for example, words like 'thank you' would be reserved for situations where the words literally and sincerely mean that one appreciates something that somebody has done, and the expression 'thank you' would not usually be used acknowledge minor favours or where people are only doing the task expected of them.

One should be aware that many, if not most, religions have dress codes which should be observed before entering their particular places of worship. There are some where it is an essential part of their rites and traditions to remove one's shoes. Usually one is made aware of this either through display notices or by the custodians of such sites. Similar customs also prevail in secular setting in South East Asia, in countries such as Myanmar, Japan, Korea and Thailand, that is in places that have no religious connection or association. This could include their traditional inns (hotels) and restaurants as well as private residences. While among some non-traditionalist citizens living in modern residences in these countries such customs might not be practiced, it is advisable to be aware of these customs and to be guided by one's hosts.

When reflecting on courtesy and politeness it is interesting to contrast how Americans behave in lifts or elevators compared with Hungarians. Americans only look down, making neither eye nor verbal contact with others in the lift. A Hungarian who is in the lift treats the person coming in as a guest, pushing the floor number button for him and as he leaves the lift says, 'viszontlátásra' or 'goodbye.'

There are some societies where based on its concept of politeness, it is customary never to refuse help to strangers, almost whatever the request. This can however on occasions result in difficult situations for the person requesting such help, as he may be given inaccurate information, principally due to reluctance of the local person in his genuine desire to be helpful and not wishing to confess to lack of knowledge.

Also read

- Etiquette, customs and conventions
- Giving and receiving gifts
- Language

CULTURE

There is an old saying, that trying to understand culture is 'like a fish trying to understand water'. Culture affects everything about us and whether one looks or observes anything about oneself, be it obvious or subtle, it will be somehow related to one's culture and environment.

When asked — what is culture and how can it be defined Lord Raglan is said to have replied: 'Culture is roughly everything we do and the monkeys, don't.'

In the commercial or business sense it affects how we look at things, behave at meetings, make decisions, organise our lives and lastly, but even more importantly, how people living in other countries and in other cultures think.

The following are just a few issues influenced by culture:

- The food one typically eats
- Clothing and accessories one wears
- Ceremonies one undergoes from birth to death
- Relationship with the nuclear or extended family
- Nature and practice of religious or non-religious beliefs
- Frequency and location of body contact with people in other social groups

- Segmentation of time and managing time
- Preferred pattern of decision-making and problem-solving

Culture even affects the way football should be played. The list of topics, for all practical purposes, is almost never-ending.

The expectations which we carry within us and which we have about how things are or should be, are based on culture, and correspond to our reference points. We unconsciously relate to these reference points when we look, listen, decide and act. We know how to interpret and evaluate what we see in our own country. When we look at apparently similar situations in a foreign country and then try to relate these to our own culture based reference points, it is then that we enter uncharted waters and it is then when we may become confused. We may encounter problems and because we are operating in a different cultural environment draw the wrong conclusions and as a result make incorrect decisions.

In some societies the term culture or cultured refers to a person's way of life, their social manner and graces and usually an acquired field of knowledge such as art, and music. In the context of this book a much wider application is used and the term culture is interpreted as covering humanity's entire social heritage.

Also read

- Protocol and conventions related to official occasions

DRESS CODE AND ETIQUETTE

Business executives and officials in most countries dress conventionally and in general set much store on presenting a formal or conservative personal appearance. There are other countries where the dress code for business executives and officials is more informal and the matter of dress is treated much more casually. Appropriateness of dress to the occasion, be it a business visit, appearance in a public place such as a restaurant or visiting someone's home, is applicable to both sexes.

In those countries where business executives customarily dress in a conservative or formal style, a visitor should try to be similarly dressed. If the visitor appears in a loud, modish, very casual, or an inappropriate form of dress he may well give his host the impression that he cannot be taken seriously.

For men it includes conventions whether a suit or national dress is worn or just a shirt and trousers or shorts, whether a tie is necessary or not, whether the occasion demands a light or a dark suit.

For women it determines whether the head, face, shoulders or upper arms should or should not be covered, the length of their dress, for example whether any part of the legs may or may not be visible, if there is a requirement for long sleeves, a full-length skirt, or robe and possibly whether a hat, scarf or veil may be appropriate.

Cultural aspects of dress conventions extend even to toys. In Iran, in order to counter the perceived negative influence of the Barbie dolls, a local company markets dolls with a headscarf covering their curls and a popular doll's outfit is a full length chador which covers the doll from head to toes.

Conventions in some countries decree that men wear something on their head, even when indoors, while in other countries such practices would be considered not just curious but even impolite. If a hat is worn there are also social conventions whether it should be raised or just touched with one's fingers when meeting and leaving friends and acquaintances. There are many different customs regarding attire in religious and holy places.

In some countries during the rule of particular political regimes there may be very strict dress codes or clothing constraints. For example, a ban on the wearing of trousers, dresses, wigs and hairpieces by women, or the wearing of jackets and ties for men.

In some countries there may be a form of standardisation of outer clothing of men and women.

In some countries laws prohibit the wearing of camouflage or camo clothing, combat gear and military type apparel by civilians including visitors. At one time such countries included Ghana, Trinidad and Tobago and the Seychelles. These laws were usually created because of the existence of local insurgents and rebels.

The inclination of some visitors wearing what the locals wear, does carry a potential risk. One hears of a visitor to a country in West Africa who decided to hang a string of local beads around her neck. This caused considerable local amusement as beads are traditionally worn at the waist to hold up one's petticoat and hanging them around her neck was as good as wearing her underwear on her head.

On the subject of dress code this is an entertaining story that has passed down through the years and relates to the Italian Duke Fabrizio of Bologna. While visiting England he was required to appear before King Henry VIII and his then Queen, Anne Boleyn. It would seem that he had to dress hastily after an abrupt romantic interlude and used the flap to contain (or perhaps restrain) his nether parts while appearing before the royal couple. Queen Anne, amused at the Italian's conspicuous bulge, remarked 'Be that thine codling or art thou glad to see me?' A codling is 15th century English for either a 'small, immature apple' or 'any of several elongated greenish English cooking apples,' so we may never know if the Duke's fruit was being ridiculed or complimented. King Henry was very distressed by the whole business and assumed this bulge (from Middle French 'boulge' meaning 'leather bag' or 'curved part', or perhaps 'curved part in a leather bag') to be the latest Continental style in courtly fashions. He immediately ordered his codpieces padded in order that he did not look out of date by comparison with Duke Fabrizio, commanding, 'My codpieces must compare favourably to Bologna.' His tailors, very literal-minded fellows all, envisioned pork sausages and thus began the whole size contest that continues to this day.

Also read

- Courtesy
- Religious beliefs
- Women in business and the professions

EDUCATION

Educational systems are culture related and even if similar facts are taught and information disseminated. The way in which it is taught in various countries will be quite distinct and different. The objectives and contents of education systems are different in every country. Teaching techniques used in most industrialised countries even at the very basic educational level, are very different from the methods used in developing countries.

Not only are people are born with many different inherited talents and qualities, but thereafter education, modified by culture, influences the way people think and the way in which they remember. In some cultures educational systems place great emphasis on remembering or the verbal memory, while in others much greater emphasis is placed on how to store and retrieve information.

Management and vocational training too is culture specific both in subject matter and method of training, although in management training the authority of a small number of world famous Schools of Management is slowly influencing management training establishments around the world.

One of the most obvious way of measuring educational is the literacy rate of countries. Some claim to have a 100% rate, while others still have a very high proportion of illiteracy.

Any organisations planning training programmes for their employees, particularly in other countries must bear in mind how people in other countries are educated. They must also find out about the possible positive and negative effects which their teaching or training will have on people in other countries. This is particularly important in those countries where religion plays an influential or even dominant role in society.

On a day-to-day basis, the standards of education and literacy in a country has a bearing on a range of subjects such as — operating instruction and instructions for use, design and understanding of signs, symbols and graphics, as well as advertising and promotional material to be used. If standards of literacy and education are low it may it may be necessary to supplement and enhance basic messages and instructions with culture specific examples and illustrations, as well as avoiding subject matter which is beyond the comprehension of the people on that country. In countries with hot climate it would not be appropriate to refer to something as being 'as white as snow'. In Far Eastern countries, for example, reference to classical allusions based on Western culture heroes, deities, fairy tales and myth will be incomprehensible, just as would be the use of a Chinese or Thai quotation in the United Kingdom or France.

In most countries a sound education and academic qualifications are essential in securing a good place in government service, industry and commerce, however there are other countries where, whilst a sound education and academic qualifications might be given favourable consideration that there are other factors such as, having the right connections might carry even greater weight. One should therefore be aware of these very different perspectives when reading the (CVs) curriculum vitae and interviewing an applicant from other countries and societies for a job.

The story goes that two policemen are standing in front of a Moscow railway station. A tourist, who does not know how to speak Russian asks one of them 'Where is the university?' The policeman then says in Russian 'I don't know'. The tourist then asks the same question in English, German, Greek, Polish, all in all in ten languages. The policeman cannot answer. The tourist is upset and goes away. The other policeman then looks at his friend and says 'Did you see, that man has spoken ten languages?' The other policeman says, 'So what? Did it help him?'

Also read

- Achievements
- Class systems, caste and social structure

EMAIL, NETIQUETTE AND CYBERSPACE BEHAVIOUR

Technology influences how written and spoken language is transmitted and understood. Electronic messages sent in one format may not always be received in the identical format and this can lead to misunderstandings and errors and could result in loss of business, mission failure or financial loss.

Email has revolutionised the worldwide workplace and has increasingly become the preferred commercial vehicle for non-verbal communication. One could describe its position as being somewhere between a telephone conversation and paper based communication. In its relatively short existence email has established its own distinctive forms and conventions relating to headed stationery, opening or salutation and closing of a communication, the date format, abbreviations, spelling simplifications, jargon, slang, acronyms as well as the use of symbols and emoticons.

One should verify whether the organisation or business with which one is in communication in another country operates policies or has established any guidelines concerning emails and texting (based on computers or hand-held devices) and if this method is an acceptable way of communicating. It is also important to determine whether an email or text message will be accepted as legal evidence relating to decisions or actions, as would a postal mail letter, a memorandum, a fax or an officially certified document.

Netiquette refers to an informal but widely used set of rules and conventions for users of the electronic network. These include a wide range of do's and don'ts. It is recommended that if, for example, one is writing in English one should avoid non-standard English, slang or jargon. One should not write the whole message in capitals nor in lowercase letters. One should be aware that it is unlikely that someone whose first language is not English would understand a text message, such as — CUL8R — meaning 'see you later'. Full use should be made of the subject line so that recipients will have an precise indication of the content of the message. When using email and other electronic communication for commercial purposes with clients in other countries one should consider making use of the automatic 'Out of Office' response, if unable to make an expeditious response to an email.

Also read

- Interpreting and translating
- Language
- Signs, pictorial representations, emoticons and other symbols
- Verbal and visual presentations

ERGONOMICS AND PRODUCT DESIGN

Ergonomics

The word ergonomics is usually applied to the study of the relationship between people and their working environment. It is therefore applicable not only to the layout of controls and instrument panels in cars, aircraft, ships, agricultural and industrial equipment, but also to office equipment, to tools and appliances used in the home for example in kitchens, bathrooms and gardens and to sport and leisure equipment.

Ergonomics are also applicable to the equipment and accessories used in connection with animals for instance horses, cattle and camels irrespective of whether they are employed as working animals or used for racing, sport and other leisure activities.

Likewise while some equipment may have been empirically or scientifically designed to take into account the body size and shape of persons of a particular user group, these parameters may not be applicable in other parts of the world where people, due to different human physical attributes may, for example, be of taller or shorter stature, have arms which are longer or shorter or have a hand span which is wider or narrower.

The story is told of a European company who had been asked to tender for the supply of kitchen cooking stoves in a South East Asian country who discovered, too late, that their standard appliances which had been designed for European users were unsuitable for local use. This was because the Asian users, who usually were of shorter stature, were unable to look into the cooking pots when on their stoves, nor able to stir the contents of pans. A Japanese company was subsequently awarded this contract because their standard stoves matched the physique of end-users in the particular market.

Product design

A product or a service, even if highly successful in one's own market, may, for a wide range of reasons, which could even be culture related, be unsuitable or even unacceptable in the market in another country. The reasons for this could include the product itself and its design, but also its packaging, presentation, or marketing. It is suggested that before marketing a product or a service in another country it is advisable to undertake market research.

One should also be aware that people in different countries may use a particular piece of machinery or equipment for different purposes; and it is essential to bear this in mind when a product or a piece of equipment is designed. A bicycle, for instance, to be used (particularly in the Netherlands) as a utility vehicle for travelling to and from work needs to be a dependable piece of equipment and will be well maintained by its owner. In another industrialised country it may be bought for leisure activities including sport or to keep fit and therefore the requirements are more likely to be stylishness and fashion, rather than durability. If designed for teenagers it might require all manner of additional gizmos and gadgets. While a bicycle to be sold in a developing country where it may well be considered the equivalent of a 'work-horse' its design needs to take into account other factors such as, that it will rarely be cleaned and likely to overloaded and otherwise abused.

A Western European manufacturer of wallets had to redesign its products when it discovered that those living in its selected overseas target market were very much a cash society and that the wallets required more space for cash and less for credit cards.

The German engineering company ThyssenKrupp highlighted the effect of culture on lift design and operation. Lifts function the same all over the world — they bring their users to their intended destination as quickly as possible. As a rule lift passengers like the illusion that there is solid ground under their feet, and even in all-round glass lifts usually they do not have a transparent floor. Cultural factors however establish differences in lift features and its users behaviour. In China, there is a preference for lift walls to be marble and mirror clad to make the lift look larger. In the Arab world, direct eye contact between sexes is disapproved of as it could lead to a flirt factor; therefore lift walls have few if any mirror surfaces. Modern lifts in some countries provide entertainment. In Germany there is a liking for information such as stock markets and weather reports, while in Asian countries there is a preference for advertising. In Europe clients prefer lift cages to have matte surfaces, while in the Middle East, gold has to dazzle and marble to shimmer. A very different predicament was encountered in Israel. There, Orthodox Jews are not allowed to activate electrical devices on a Sabbath, that is from Friday evening to Saturday evening. Pressing a lift button would be an immediate violation of the Sabbath prohibition. Therefore the Israel Parliament made it obligatory to equip every new multi-story building in the country with automatic lifts and on a Sabbath, lifts remain in continuous operation and stop at every floor, without any human physical input.

Also read

- Advertising
- Colour preferences and prejudices
- Human physical differences
- Information, operating instructions and methods of use

ETHNIC STEREOTYPING

Almost everybody has a mental picture or impressions of members of other ethnic groups, races and nationalities, very often even before they have actually met them face-to-face. These views are based on the way in which other people are portrayed and based on many different sources, not in the least by the way they are portrayed in pulp fiction and the mass media. Such views are even more distorted during the periods of conflict, be they cold or hot wars.

Sources for these impressions include languages where there are a wide range of expressions suggesting the presence of specific traits in particular ethnic, racial and other groups. In the English language for example, these include 'Chinese puzzle', 'Dutch treat', and 'to take French leave', the idiomatic translation of this when spoken in French is '*filer à l'Anglaise*', or 'to take English leave'.

The very fact that many people believe that these expressions contain an element of truth shows the danger of accepting them at face value. There is little doubt that many are based on long forgotten historical facts, but many may be, at this point in time and for that reason many decades or even centuries later, somewhat out of date and probably inaccurate. It is therefore essential to bear in mind that even an unconscious acceptance of these impressions can create misunderstandings, well before any face-to-face meetings takes place.

Also read

- Attitudes

Etiquette, Customs and Conventions

Books and guides were written on these subjects by mediaeval courtiers as long ago as during the time of the Egyptian Pharaohs. Since then many more such books have been published, not only by those responsible for protocol in governments and international organisations, but also by writers of social columns in newspapers and magazines.

The range of subjects includes guidelines as to personal behaviour and manners, dress, conversation and just about every human activity from conception to burial, and are therefore relevant to most of the activities, actions and circumstances described in this book.

One definition, attributed to Confucius, states that if there was a correct mode of behaviour prescribed for every possible situation, the everyday stress and grind of human contacts would, as it were, be oiled to everybody's benefit.

There are a number of languages, for example, French and German, which have two different forms of address for 'you'. The more intimate form of these is usually used only among members of the family and among close friends, while the other is the more generally used form. Rules vary and it depends very much on the social environment and status of the people concerned. It is important to realise, particularly by those who live in countries where there is a much greater degree of informality in business and official circles, not to use the more familiar terms unless invited to do so by the other party. Similarly one should wait to be asked before getting on a first-name basis in countries where both first names and family names are in use.

As to who should walk first through a door or into or out of a lift often results in an amusing confusion with each party saying the equivalent of 'no — after you' and trying to persuade the other to take the first step. Good manners might suggest that the visitor or the more senior person should take precedence, but this too is based on local, culture related conventions. Likewise local culture determines whether a woman precedes a man when walking through a door and when getting into or out of a car or taxi.

While etiquette is a code that governs the expectation of social behaviour *'savoir faire'* is the instinctive ability to know how to deal with any situation that arises. There is the story of three Frenchmen who were asked what is meant by savoir faire. The first one answers — a man comes home and finds his wife in the arms of another man. If the husband then says nothing, turns around, closes the door and leaves — that is French savoir faire. The second Frenchman then says, 'Well, you have almost explained it, but not quite. A man comes home and finds his wife in the arms of another man. He says: 'Excuse me, please continue'. He then turns around, closes the door and leaves — that is real French savoir faire'. The third Frenchman then says, 'Gentlemen — well that's almost, but still not absolutely right. When the man comes home and finds his wife in the arms of another man. He says: 'Excuse me, please continue'. He then turns around, closes the door and leaves. Now if the other man can continue, that is proper French savoir faire.'

Also read

- Courtesy
- Manners, conduct and behaviour

FLOWERS AND GIVING FLOWERS

Floral gifts are a suitable gift for many business and social occasions. Flowers are available in various forms including cut flowers in bunches or bouquets as well as in more formal arrangements and in flower baskets. Then there are pot plants, ornamental foliage, and wreaths. Also available in many different formats are artificial flowers and while they can be both beautiful and expensive, as a gift they may not be considered right and proper by people in some countries.

When giving flowers one should also bear in mind considerations such as whether they are to be hand-delivered or to be sent by a florist. If sent, there are culture related traditions which determine whether they should arrive before the event or afterwards.

Conventions as to what type of flowers or floral arrangements are to be sent, as a 'thank you' after an event, such as a social or a business dinner, is very much culture-related. Such culture related factors determine whether to give flowers, foliage or plants. Other factors of significance include — species, colour, number of individual stems, blooms or flowers, whether they are to be presented unwrapped or wrapped and if wrapped whether in plain or coloured paper or clear film wrapping. Furthermore whether ribbon should be used and if so, the appropriate colour of the ribbon. Lastly whether the floral gift is to be accompanied by a card and the style of message.

In all countries flowers are symbolic and express or communicate genuine situations. Great care should be taken to avoid sending inappropriate flowers as a thank you gift for dinner or for other events. In most countries there are floral conventions and there are even special floral dictionaries explaining the meaning of individual flowers. Unfortunately national conventions do sometime contradict one another, for example where in one country lavender can mean distrust and in another it signifies pleasant memories.

In almost all countries there are flowers that are directly associated with death and funerals. In France, Hungary, Italy and Poland for instance chrysanthemums are associated with funerals and memorial days and more or less signify death. In China white and yellow chrysanthemums have the same significance. Similarly in the Philippines white flowers are taboo and should only be given when attending a funeral. Blue flowers however represent wealth and are generally impressive but should not be coupled with yellow which represents jealousy. Orchids are appreciated as they symbolize longevity.

In many countries, if cut flower bouquets are given as a present there should be an uneven number of stems and never number 13, as this number is considered unlucky. Germany is one of the countries where this particular custom is relevant. In Italy the unlucky number of stems is 17, while 13 stems are considered lucky. Then there are some countries where the custom of uneven numbers of stems only applies if there are less than nine stems and still others where the arrangement of uneven number of stems only applies to roses. In Russia when flowers are given they should be in bouquets containing an uneven number, except at funerals. Sending plants to the elderly persons in Japan is not customary, since some still believe that a gift of plants will make the illness 'take root'.

Before sending flowers as gifts to someone in foreign country it is always advisable to seek advice from a florist in that country, to avoid misunderstanding or perhaps even giving offence.

Also read

- Giving and receiving gifts
- Signs, pictorial representations, emoticons and other symbols
- Taboos, superstitions and non-religious beliefs

Food, Drink and Eating Lifestyle

Religious beliefs affect consumption of some foods, alcoholic drinks and beverages. Additionally there are also climatic, environmental, economic and culture related factors which influence peoples attitudes to the cultivation, growing, harvesting, storage, transportation and preparation of food, drink and beverages.

People in some countries like hot spicy food, as for example, some of those living in parts of the Indian subcontinent and South East Asia, while those living in other regions might prefer food with more subtle flavours and taste. There are for example those in

Western Europe who like strong smelling and strong tasting cheese who, under no circumstances what-so-ever would eat an equally strong smelling South East Asian tropical fruit like Durian, and the reverse also applies. There are those who are entirely vegan by choice and not necessarily for any religious reasons, while there are others who are vegetarians.

Some people consider a dish made with the meat of dogs a delicacy, while others would equate eating dogmeat with cannibalism. Pork, horsemeat and the meat of donkeys are among other products where definite views are held by those in favour and those against its consumption. In almost all circumstances these attitudes are based either on culture related whims of human taste or on religious principles. Nobody knows why one species of animal is favoured as a source of meat for inhabitants of one country, whilst to those in another it is considered a taboo animal, that is judged to be unclean. Although the pig was considered an unclean animal in Ancient Egypt, during the period around 2,800 BC pork was allowed to be eaten on certain days when these animals were sacrificed to Bacchus and Luna and it is still not clear how these taboos originated and how rigorously they were observed.

There are still in this day and age, large areas in Central Africa and Eastern Asia, where there is no tradition of milking animals and many adults in these countries are physiologically unable to absorb lactose which is a main constituent of fresh milk.

Packaging of beer is sometimes both culture and climate related. In Jamaica and Taiwan there is a demand for beer packed in small 20 cl (centilitre) bottles, to counter the concern that beer in larger bottles will get warm, before the contents can be consumed.

In the United States consumers buy green bananas and wait till they ripen, while in Japan people only buy ripe bananas. One of the main reasons for this being that consumers in the USA have larger living accommodation and therefore tend to shop just once a week, while Japanese who live in much smaller household, buy on a daily basis.

In many countries, particularly in the larger countries, there are often regional and local preferences relating to food, drink and beverages. These include factors such as taste, flavour, smell, aroma, colour, texture, consistency and portion size. It is therefore unwise, particularly from a commercial standpoint, to generalise about national food habits, except in relation to specific produce and products.

A tale of a culinary culture shock relates an incident in the canteen of a Japanese car assembly plant in the North-East of England. A Japanese manager on a visit to the plant was seen filling his plate with rice and barbecued chicken. He then proceeded to the dessert counter and asked for a portion of custard to be poured over the food. The serving staff told him very politely that this was not the use for which the custard was intended. However the Japanese visitor persisted and the chef was called. The chef explained that a dessert or sweet item should not be mixed with a main course. So why, asked the Japanese, did the canteen serve a peach slice with pork and a ring of pineapple with the gammon. There being no answer to such logic the chef with a sigh poured the custard over the rice and chicken.

Many cultural behaviours can be witnessed during the physical act of eating and drinking which relate to formal and non-formal eating occasions as well as to snacking. These cultural factors are associated with — how dining tables are laid, the type of utensils used for eating and drinking which includes crockery, cutlery and glasses, the layout of menu cards and wine lists, how food and drink is served, in what sequence it is served, how it is consumed and lastly how eating utensils are positioned to indicate that one has finished one's meal. It also includes conventions on how one should and shouldn't express appreciation for food and drink, such as belching during or after a meal.

Also read

- Business entertaining
- Table etiquette and eating
- Taboos, superstitions and non-religious beliefs

FORMS OF ADDRESS AND USE OF TITLES

Each country has its particular forms of etiquette and protocol concerning modes of address, both verbal and in writing, for addressing the head of state, government ministers, central, provincial and local government officials, the clergy, the judiciary, those in the armed forces, the police, in universities and other educational establishments. In some countries there may also be appropriate forms of address and titles for those engaged at various levels of management in commerce and industry, and it would be considered a serious breach of good manners if one did not use the appropriate titles. In France and Germany professional titles are usually used in conjunction with normal titles, for example Monsieur le Directeur, or Herr Direktor. In this context one's guideline should be — make free use of titles of respect rather than running the risk of not using enough and thereby falling short of what is due and fitting, particularly so in those countries where considerable emphasis is laid on use of titles and honorifics.

Although in most countries a person's name is prefaced with a title, as for example in English-speaking countries where the man's name is prefaced by the word Mister. There are other countries, such as Turkey, where the title Bey for a man is used as a suffix and mentioned after the family name, for example Yesilay Bey. In Thailand a person's name is normally preceded by *Khun*, the equivalent of Mr, Mrs or Miss, unless the bearer of the name possesses a higher title. All Thai people have two legal names, a personal name which comes first and a family name which comes last. People are introduced by the first name only which is preceded by Khun. In Austria it is customary for a wife to be addressed by the professional title of her husband, and the wife of Herr Dr. Braun would be addressed as Frau Dr. Braun and not as Frau Braun. In Italy the courtesy title *'Dottore'* or 'Doctor' is often used particularly when unsure about someone's professional status.

Business and professional titles and designations often have very different significance, meaning or status in other countries and societies. It should not therefore be assumed that the designation or title of a person in another country has a similar status or level of responsibility as would a person with the same title or designation in one's own country. The status or level of responsibility of that person may be the same but could well be superior or inferior, this conundrum can only be resolved by means of subtle communication.

Also read

- Business cards
- Conversation and communication
- Greeting, introductions, modes of address and leave taking
- Names
- Women in business and the professions

GESTURES

Gestures, meaning the use of body language, support and supplement the spoken language. Gestures do not have the same meaning the whole world over and minor or even major misunderstandings occur where they differ. It has often been suggested that visitors to foreign countries should learn about their gestures or non-verbal communication, just as they would learn the local language, particularly since one can, even unintentionally, cause offence by making an inappropriate or disrespectful gesture or sign. It should also be noted that since gestures vary from culture to culture and from country to country and there are many which, if made in another country, might not signify anything and just like a strange language will be unintelligible to the person with whom one is trying to communicate.

Worldwide there are literally hundreds of different gestures. The American gesture of slitting one's throat means 'I love you' in

Swaziland. Even in Western Europe the list of meaningful gestures total several dozens and include ear touching, thumbs-up, nose tap, the V-sign, and the OK sign with thumb and forefinger touching in a circle.

In some countries beckoning or signalling to someone to come closer is done with the palm facing upwards, while in other countries it is executed with the palm facing downwards. This particular gesture often confuses visitors from those countries where this gesture or hand signal is used for waving goodbye to someone who is leaving.

While pointing at objects with the forefinger is the norm in some countries, it is wholly totally unacceptable or taboo in others, where this should be done with the thumb, or the whole hand, or with the head combined with an opening and closing or pouting of the lips, or the chin.

Tapping the temple or the side of the forehead, or alternatively screwing the forefinger against it is an insult signal indicating stupidity or worse in some countries, while in the Netherlands tapping the temple means intelligence and their sign for stupidity is the tapping of the centre of the forehead.

Also read

- Body language and non-verbal communication
- Cars and driving

GIVING AND RECEIVING GIFTS

The niceties of gift etiquette depend on the conventions, customs and official guidelines of a country. Even within a country different conventions may apply depending on whether gifts are to be given to a government official, a business executive or in a purely social context.

When deciding to give a gift to someone in other country some questions need to be asked: What is the purpose of the gift? Who is to be the recipient? Is there a possibility of the recipient misinterpreting the gift? What kind of gift is appropriate? How is it to be wrapped? What is the occasion? How is the gift to be given? Who will be giving the gift? All this will involve research to avoid giving unintentional offence.

In countries where it is inappropriate to give gifts to a person within an establishment, it may be more appropriate, if this is acceptable, that the gift is given to the person's organisation.

In countries and societies marked by enormous gaps between rich and poor, gifts as acts of generosity often demonstrate status. To withhold gifts is to deny the affluence and prosperity of the superior person. It may therefore an advantage to one's position particularly if that person is a representative of an organisation to demonstrate his status by displaying generosity. Further reference to this is made under Bribery and Corruption.

As to what is and what is not a gift, can only be established by those involved. One must also be aware that the implication the giver of a gift is trying to convey may not, for culture related reasons, be the same as understood by the recipient of the gift. The statement 'If there is no compromise of business or personal interests by either party in the exchange, it is a gift', is too simple. It is sometimes said that whereas the interest of persons from a Western culture country is to do business and that from this a personal relationship may evolve, while people from non-Western cultures seek, initially, to establish a personal relationship from which a business relationship may develop. It is also believed that while persons living in Western culture countries seek to discharge obligations through an exchange of gifts, while persons in non-Western culture countries are more likely to create them, is perhaps more realistic.

The practice of pre-giving, that is, the presentation of a gift to a person early on in their relationship, even at their initial meeting is well established in the culture of some countries, as for example, in Japan. Its purpose is by and large completely genuine, in that it seeks to create a favourable atmosphere and establish a positive relationship between the participants. However in some countries and cultures its purpose may be to establish an obligation, by means of which the recipient of a gift will be more amenable to requests by the giver. A classic example of this is being invited to sit down after entering a carpet shop in a souk in the Middle East and then being offered a cup of coffee. Although this is a most pleasing gesture its objective is to generate the right atmosphere for a subsequent purchase.

To return a gift is usually considered an affront, but there may be instances when it may be better to return a gift than to accept it, particularly when the recipient has no possibility nor intention of doing a favour in return.

One should be very careful to select a gift, appropriate to the occasion. On the one hand it should not be too expensive while on the other it should not be too inconsequential or trivial. Deciding on a gift involves a delicate balance of fine-tuning the value of the gift to the occasion.

There are a number of countries where, based on myth and superstition, it is unacceptable to give a knife as a present, be it a kitchen knife, pocket knife or any other kind of knife. In Japan, for example, it signifies bringing bad luck. In the United Kingdom there is a myth which claims that to give someone a knife will lead to the relationship being cut or severed, unless the recipient gives the giver a coin in return. An opposite belief exists in Finland, where giving someone a knife, particularly a hunting knife, is a sign of trust.

If invited into a person's home in many Middle Eastern countries, one's host would feel most insulted if the gift was food or drink. It would suggest that the host is probably not hospitable nor generous.

In countries where consumption of alcohol is forbidden, it would obviously be inappropriate to give any kind of alcoholic beverage as a gift, including any confectionery or other food product that may contain alcohol. Giving a handkerchief as a gift to a person living in a South American country or to a person in China would not be appropriate since handkerchiefs are associated with sadness and grief, as they are often given to mourners at funerals. Similarly giving a clock to someone in China is inappropriate since in Mandarin Chinese the words for 'to give a clock' have an identical tone or meaning as 'to escort someone to their death'. In Japan a present depicting a picture of a badger would not be suitable since a badger is the symbol of cunning. If one intends to give flowers to one's hosts one should find out about local customs and convention, particularly whether bouquets of flowers should comprise an even or uneven number of stems.

To the Chinese happiness is 'born a twin', and gifts should always come in pairs. When giving a gift to someone living in India it should be in an uneven number particularly when money is given as a present, and one would, for example, add a Rs 10 (ten rupee) banknote to a Rs 100 banknote to make it Rs 110.

In a number of South East Asian countries including Korea, Malaysia, Singapore and the Philippines, one of the reasons given for wrapping gifts as well as for not opening a gift in front of others is to avoid a situation in which the recipient may feel disappointed or embarrassed. In countries where this custom prevails, the recipient of a wrapped gift may well put it aside and only open it after the guests have left. There may however be circumstances where one is urged to open the wrapped gift even when the donor and others are present, and it is then essential to accept it with sincerely felt pleasure.

In some countries the wrapping of a gift is as important as the gift itself. In Germany, for example, great value is placed on quality and appearance of the wrapping. In China one must not use a white gift wrapper as the colour is associated with death. In India and in Japan a combination of black and white for gift wrapping is to be avoided, as this colour combination is usually reserved for funerals. During the 1980's it was reported in some newspapers, that a foreign airline was seeking the landing rights at Tokyo airport. Thereafter there were rumours that the airline lost its bid because it had presented the Japanese negotiators with gifts wrapped in white paper tied with black ribbon. It took the airline several more years to obtain landing rights.

In addition to conventional exchanges of gifts there are in every country many different occasions, often traditional, for gift-giving, not only to family and friends but also to colleagues and employees. These events include many different religious and secular occasions. There are seasonal festivals which include Christmas, St Nicholas Day, Santa Claus and New Year celebrations. While other gift-giving occasions include — betrothals or engagements, weddings and wedding anniversaries, birthdays and in some countries Name days or Saints' days, graduation celebrations, promotion, retirement and recovery from an illness.

Also read

- Bribery and corruption
- Business entertaining
- Flowers and giving flowers
- Taboos, superstitions and non-religious beliefs

GREETING CARDS

In many countries it is customary to send greeting cards containing messages of goodwill to business colleagues and friends on special occasions which include secular festivals like New Year and religious festivals like Christmas. When sending cards to a person in a foreign country it should be borne in mind that the recipient may be of a different religious persuasion or of none, and it is essential to ensure that appropriate text or wording is used. One should for example when sending a Christmas card or a New

Year card to someone who is not a Christian and does not live in a Christian country use more appropriate words. Such words could be: 'Greetings', 'With the Season's Greetings' or 'Thinking of you'. Similarly pictorial representations should be chosen with care to take into account the particular person's, the country's and its peoples' perceptions, prejudices and regulations concerning symbols, signs, images of the human form or that of animals.

One should be aware that greeting cards used in those countries where the language is written from right to left may be printed and expected to be read in this particular type of format, for example, the front of a two page card is the right outside cover and not the left outside cover, as it would be in Western culture countries.

Similar comments apply to greeting messages sent by electronic means such as by fax or via the internet.

Also read

- Religious beliefs
- Signs, pictorial representations, emoticons and other symbols

GREETING, INTRODUCTIONS, MODES OF ADDRESS AND LEAVE-TAKING

Greeting

Hand-shaking is the most usual form of greeting among both men and women in Europe, North, Central and South America. However how frequently people do shake hands when meeting, greeting and leaving, varies from country to country. In Belgium, as well as many of the Spanish speaking South American countries, one would shake hands with just about everyone at almost every meeting and also on taking leave.

In other countries, for instance India, Myanmar and Thailand, a man would not shake hands with a woman unless she extended her hand, first.

There are innumerable conventions as to whether handshakes should be accompanied with a slight bow of the head, be firm and resolute rather than in a form of a light contact, whether it would be only with one's fingers rather than the whole hand, or whether the hand is pumped up and down. There is for example a traditional African handshake practised in East Africa, and learning and copying this extended form of greeting demonstrates an understanding of one's host's tradition. Handshakes may be very prolonged and in some countries the host may continue to hold a visitor's hand as he leads him into his office or his house. The best advice under all these circumstances is to be pragmatic and to respond to the host's initiative.

In a few Central European countries when a man meets and greets a woman, a hand-kiss might take the place of a handshake.

In some countries, male colleagues and male friends greet each other with close hugs and embraces, instead of shaking hands or bowing, they may also greet each other by kissing. There are many other forms of greeting including, in Asia and South East Asia where each person's hands are folded by placing both palms at chest height and is then accompanied either with a nod of the head or a bow. The Japanese use very complex and ritualised forms of greeting and leave-taking and where the level of formality is appropriate to the persons involved and their respective status.

There is the tale of the occasion when two foreign office officials were at a London airport awaiting the arrival of a government minister from a lesser known foreign country. Just as the door to the hospitality lounge was opened the junior official turned to his colleague and asked, 'Now what do we do? Do we shake hands or rub noses?'

Introductions

In most Western culture countries conventions regarding formal introduction recommend that the more important person is addressed first, in Thailand however, conventions are different and the inferior person is addressed first. There are also some countries where introductions are not a traditional practice, but nothing prevents one asking for somebody's name and giving one's own name.

Modes of Address

It is important to use the correct form of address when addressing officials or business executives, whether verbally or in writing, and in many countries there are numerous customs and convention regarding the way a person should be addressed either verbally or in writing.

In some countries persons are addressed by their family or surname, while in others only the first or given name is used. In the United Kingdom Mr John Smith and Mrs Julie Brown would be addressed as Mr Smith and Mrs Brown, but in many South East Asian countries and in several of the South American countries, for example, the correct mode of address would be Mr John and Mrs Julie.

In most Spanish speaking countries in Europe and South America the double surname or family name system, incorporating both paternal and maternal family names, is applied. In all cases, the paternal family name is shown first followed by the maternal family name. However, both in speech and in correspondence a person would only be addressed by their first family name that is Senor Juan Gomez Sanchez would be addressed as Senor Gomez and not as Senor Sanchez. Women too have two family names, and on marriage would maintain these and add their husbands' paternal family to these, therefore the wife of Senor Gomez whose unmarried name was Senora Maria Molina Lopez, would become Senora Maria Molina Lopez de Gomez, generally however she would be addressed as Senora de Gomez.

In Brazil where the national language is Portuguese, the last family name is used which is contrary to Spanish practice, and Dr Paulo Lopes Pereira would normally be referred to as Dr Pereira, but often Brazilians are known by their first name only that is Dr Paulo.

In some countries women retain their maiden name after marriage and married couples may well have different family names, while their children's names could incorporate both family names.

In some countries such as China and the Hong Kong Special Administrative Region, the family name is the first name and the second and other names are the given names, thus Mr Hu Ting-Yi is Mr Hu. Many businesspeople in Hong Kong have adopted a European style of writing of their name and Mr Wong Man Ying or Mr Wong might well be Mr M.Y. Wong.

In Myanmar, for example, there is no system of first and family name and when speaking to a local person, the full name is invariably used. Also in Myanmar, wives retain their own names and children do not take their parents name.

In Iceland, although there are some exceptions, a person's name is their forename, to which is appended their father's name. A man whose forename is Stefan and whose father's forename was Magnus would be known as Stefan Magnusson.

In different cultures there are various pronouns which are used to address another person and how one translates and uses the word 'you', for example, depends on the relationship between the two persons concerned, and also whether the other person is a relative, an intimate friend, a business colleague or an official. One should not presume to use a more intimate form of speech, unless invited to do so by the other person or advised by someone acquainted with local etiquette.

In practically every country a wide range of different professional and deferential titles and honorifics are used. Such marks of respect, however phrased, are appreciated everywhere and readily reciprocated, and if in doubt, it is better to be respectful.

In some countries the same title or prefix is applied to both single and married women, in others each has a distinctive prefix, in yet others different forms of address or titles for men and women do not exist, and both are addressed with the same title.

Leave-taking

In most countries conventions for leave-taking, after taking into account that the words used will probably be different, usually correspond to those used for greeting.

Also read

- Forms of address and use of titles
- Male-Female relationships

Hours of Work

When planning visits and appointments in a foreign country one should take into consideration factors such as hours of work, religious and secular festivals and annual holidays.

Most commercial organisations in Western culture countries operate on a five day basis but some still work a five and half-day week. In these countries the working week is from Monday to Saturday and Sunday is considered the day of rest. In many Western culture countries those who are described as professionals which would include accountants, architects, bankers, lawyers, stockbrokers, journalists, as well as local and central government officials usually work a five day week, from Monday to Friday. Usually most retail outlets are open on a Saturday and increasingly for a limited number of hours on a Sunday. There is a trend in a few countries for some financial offices, for example banks, to be open on a six day week basis.

In countries where the official day of rest is Friday, for example in most of the Muslim countries, the working week is from Saturday to Thursday. In Israel, where Saturday is the day of rest, the working week runs from Sunday to midday of Friday.

Customs and practices regarding opening hours of retail outlets, as well as commercial and administrative offices on religious and on secular Official Public Holidays vary from country to country. In many countries the day prior to a Public Holiday is either a full or a half day of rest, when many businesses and offices are closed.

There is no common characteristic regarding hours of work during a working day which in any case is usually different for the various professions and occupations, for example those working in the emergency services, seafarers and aircrews. In some countries work starts around 07.00h and finishes early; in other countries offices open around 09.30h. Climatic factors such as winter or summer, the wet and dry seasons, the hot and the cold seasons and hours of daylight have a bearing on this. Each country has its favoured annual holiday periods for both employers and employees, and there is usually a co-relation between the geographical location of the country and seasonal weather patterns.

Mealtimes too vary from country to country, and within a country between its regions. Some have midday meal breaks starting at 11.00h others as late as 15.00h. The duration of midday breaks can be as long as four hours, and might include a 'siesta' period. When the midday meal break is late, that is around 15.00h, one may find that the morning working period could be as long as 7 to 8 hours. Just as in the case of hours of work, seasonal and/or climate changes may alter mealtimes and eating patterns.

Also read

- Appointments
- National or public holidays and festivals both secular and religious

Human Physical Differences

The world is populated by many different races and predominant groups include Caucasoid, Mongoloid, Negroid and Asian Indian and a broad range of distinctive physical features distinguish these groups from one another including body shape and dimension. These features include height, body weight, hand length, sitting height, head size and shape, skin colour and tone, and hair characteristics such as colour, calibre or diameter, also hair shape for example straight, wavy, curly or frizzled.

Even after making due allowance for differences in the size and shape of people based on sex and age, there are various items of attire, clothing, sport and leisure clothes and protective clothing which, even if they fit members of one race, may not fit members of another.

It is acknowledged, that men in the United Kingdom are shorter and weigh less than men in the United States and that women in the United Kingdom are taller and weigh less than those in the USA.

A British manufacturer of men's belts which were to be worn with trousers had to modify his products for the Japanese market as Japanese men had much slimmer waists.

In addition to dissimilarities between different races and groups there are also differences in body shape within many of the major racial groups, such differences, for example, of their hands and feet which not only have a bearing on size but also have an effect on the shape and form of gloves and of footwear.

Head sizes and shapes differ from country to country. The largest heads are to be found in Germany and the smallest in Far Eastern countries. With regard to shape, they can be either oval or round. People in Western countries have a more oval shape, while those in Eastern countries have a rounder head. This means that a hat designed for a European probably does not fit an Asian person properly and vice-versa and if a hat made for a person from a different ethnic or racial group is worn, it might well look odd or peculiar on the head of a person from another ethnic group.

Also read

- Dress code and etiquette
- Ergonomics and design of products
- Units of measure

INFORMATION, OPERATING INSTRUCTIONS AND METHODS OF USE

Almost everybody who has visited a foreign country has come across notices, restaurant menus and instructions with curious expressions ranging from the sheer amusing to the incomprehensible. A department store in a city in an Asian country announced 'Visit our bargain basement, one flight up'; the announcement in the English language advertising donkey rides for tourists which stated 'Would you like to ride on your ass?' and a menu which advertised 'cream dognuts' instead of doughnuts.

The growth and development of international trade has resulted in increased exports of items including domestic appliances, office machinery and factory equipment to countries where other languages are spoken. Service manuals containing instructions for use often accompany these goods. A Japanese car exported to England in 1965 contained the following instructions 'If the brakes should fail, stop immediately and drive to the nearest garage'. However, unintelligible or simply poor or bad translations can not only cause problems, but can sometimes lead to disastrous results, particularly if complex or dangerous equipment or products are involved.

One hears of a federal law in the United States which stated that the following notice must be affixed to roller towels in public places. 1. Pull the towel gently with both hands. 2. Wipe hands and face. 3. WARNING: Do not attempt to hang from the towel, or insert your head into the towel loop. Failure to follow these simple instructions can be harmful or injurious.

Because people's background may be completely different and since not all are literate even very simple descriptions or instructions may not be understood. Quite often pictorial representations are applied to the outer packaging of goods destined for foreign markets, for example the picture of raindrops falling on an umbrella which indicates that the package should not be exposed to rain. But even such symbols and/or pictorial representation might not be understood by persons living in another culture or society. It is therefore essential to take into account the literacy as well as the culture of the country where the product or service is to be used or operated.

In some countries the information desk facility at airports, railway stations and on motorways are sign-posted with the letter 'I', in others it is identified with a large question mark or even two question marks, one upright and the other inverted.

Imprecise terms such as 'teaspoon full', 'half a soup spoon', 'a cup full' are capable of many different interpretations, a Chinese soup spoon is very different in size and capacity from a soup spoon used in Germany or the United Kingdom.

It would seem obvious that anyone exporting equipment would ensure that the accompanying instructions had been translated into the language of the importing country. This would not appear to be universal, because in the mid-1980s the Saudi Arabian authorities stated that all instructions for use accompanying any industrial and electro-domestic machinery must be in Arabic as well as any other language that a manufacturer chooses to include. While this instruction was not mandatory, one might well find that goods without instructions in Arabic could be discriminated against.

Packaging is another area where it is essential to be aware of culture difference on the part of consumers. When, European brewers exported bottled beer to the United States, they learned that in some States there is a custom of cooling beers in buckets of ice. To resolve the problem of labels from sliding off bottles the company had to use a special bonding agent or adhesive.

An American food manufacturer exporting to Japan succeeded in offending his potential Japanese consumers by printing the following words on packs of ready-to-cook products 'As easy to cook as rice'. In a country where rice preparation is regarded as a skilled art, these words were, at the very least, counter-productive and to stimulate sales, the packaging had to be redesigned.

There are many goods, products and items of equipment which in another country may well be used for purposes different from their use or utilisation in the country where they have been grown, processed or manufactured. In most of the industrialised Western culture countries a bicycle might well be bought as a piece of keep-fit equipment, as a leisure-time item, for sport or as a child's toy. On the other hand in the Netherlands a bicycle is more frequently used as a utility vehicle for travelling to and from work, while in a developing country it might well be used primarily as a 'work-horse' to transport produce and products. It is important to be aware that almost every end-user market may have different product requirements which need to be reflected in the design of the product, in subsequent promotional activities, as well as in arrangements for service and maintenance of such products.

Even laundry washing powders and detergents need to take into account cultural differences. Clothing stains in the south of Europe are different from those in Northern Europe, for example Scandinavian food stains, because the Spanish and Italians eat different foods, and there are special problems associated with stains caused by olive oil and tomatoes.

Even in Europe there are some items of domestic electrical equipment where both weather and cultural difference effect the design of equipment. For example in hot, dry countries washing machines have a much lower spin speeds than in cold, wet climate and countries, where the typical spin speed is 1,200 rpm. In Spain, the average spin speed is 600 rpm, and it is unlikely that one could sell a washing machine with that spin speed in the United Kingdom.

Also read

- Advertising
- Ergonomics and product design
- Signs, pictorial representations, emoticons and other symbols
- Units of measure

INTERPRETING AND TRANSLATING

Interpreting

When visiting other countries, one should remember that it is the visitor who is the foreigner and it would therefore be more courteous and polite to try to talk at least initially in language of the host country.

When speaking in their second or foreign language, some people may use a foreign word but at the same time retain the effective meaning of this word in their native or mother tongue, at least until they are also able to think in the second language. There is therefore always a possibility that these persons will not be speaking with the same meaning even when they are conversing in their second language. This can be particularly so when the foreign language was learned in an artificial environment such as a classroom.

If one is unable to speak a foreign language, it is usually advisable to employ an interpreter unless the host offers to speak the language of the visitor. If interpretation is required it is better to engage one's own interpreter, since in some situations it can be assumed that that the interpreter may not necessarily be a neutral or disinterested party.

When an interpreter is used it is courteous, even during the translating process, to look at the person with whom one is conversing and if appropriate in that country make eye contact, and not look at the interpreter. One should also try, whenever possible, to keep ideas compact, sentences short and make the time of one's presentation about half the normal length.

One point which must be kept in mind is that very few interpreters, no matter how experienced they may be, have in-depth knowledge in every area of expertise. It is therefore prudent, if at all possible, to have an orientation meeting with the interpreter prior to a business meeting or a conference.

A speaker at an international conference once told an appalling racist joke, and after a delay to allow for simultaneous translation there was an appreciative laugh from the audience. When a fellow speaker who could understand the language of the speaker, later commented on this to the translator he was told, 'I dislike the joke as much as you. I therefore said to the audience — the speaker has just told a very unpleasant joke that I am not prepared to translate for you. However, for the sake of appearances and so that he knows that you have not gone to sleep, would you please laugh now!'

At an International conference, after listening to a particularly vociferous, lengthy and uninterrupted tirade delivered by Stalin, Churchill is said to have whispered to his interpreter: 'What is the old boy saying?' To which the interpreter replied:
'He says — No!'

It should be noted that a number of international organisations, for instance divisions of the United Nations Organisation, have a number of *official* languages but usually operate in a more limited number of *working* languages.

Translating

Practically all normal text is capable of being translated in so far as it conveys information which can be converted into another language. Translations even when accurate, may still involve some loss of nuance and tone. On the other hand it can also result in improvement as for example in poetry when it is translated successfully, because this not only involves language but also the music and rhythm of poetry. There is a politically incorrect and chauvinist adage about translations which asserts: 'Translations are like women, if they are faithful they are probably not beautiful and if they are beautiful they are probably not faithful.'

It is essential that when written material is translated, particularly where technical matters are concerned, that it is accurate. All translation work has its pitfalls, but these are multiplied many times over with technical copy. Languages are not static and translators should therefore be up-to-date in the current written idiom, as well as in the specialist technology. To retain the services of translators who may have left their country many years or even decades ago is usually fraught with danger. It is not likely to improve the sales of a company's latest scientific piece of equipment if its sales brochure has been translated in the style of a 19th Century author.

To guard against misunderstandings translations should always be checked and proof-read by a second independent linguist, and under certain circumstances it is advisable to have the translated foreign text re-translated into the original language by another translator and the results compared with the original.

To increase speed and reduce costs the use of machine translation, also described as computer-aided translation, has increased. While this method may be faster and cheaper than human translators, it is also more prone to errors and blunders. This brings to mind two examples. In one document the phrase 'out of sight, out of mind' was translated into 'blind idiot'. In another manuscript translated for presentation at a German engineering conference, reference was made to an 'aquatic male ram', which when compared with the original text turned out to be a hydraulic ram. Fortunately someone corrected the translations by having the foreign text re-translated into English.

An example of the problems one can encounter just by using capital letters in the wrong place, or worse still, by not using them at all is the German language sentence *'Ich habe in Berlin liebe Genossen'* meaning 'I have dear comrades in Berlin'. If the capital letters of the two words *Liebe* and *Genossen* are switched and the message reads *'Ich habe in Berlin Liebe genossen'* it then means 'I have enjoyed making love in Berlin'.

People enjoy taking liberty with terms and expressions in a foreign language, none more so than the British. The British levity with the French language can be illustrated as follows:

'coup de gras' — a French lawnmower;
'pas de deux' — a father of twins;
'mal de mer' — sick of one's mother;
'pièce de resistance' — a young lady who fights off unwelcome advances;
'metronome' — a little man who lives on the Paris Underground.

Translating particular words accurately from one language to another is sometimes virtually impossible. It is most unlikely that all words in a language which have been written in its own particular script, characters or ideograms will be absolutely correct when translated and this is the reason why there are often many different written and spoken versions of what should be the same name, be it of persons, companies, streets or towns. This is due to the fact that when some languages such as Chinese, Japanese and Korean are converted into Latin script there is often more than one system of romanisation and this results in confusion. Examples of this can be found when a name in the Thai language and script is translated into English and written in Latin script, or an Arabic name which has been translated and then written in Chinese, and likewise conversely.

Sometimes, as for example in Chinese, there is more than one translation system. The name of the former Chinese leader can be written as 'Mao Zedong' using the Pinyin romanisation system, or 'Mao Tse-tung' using the Wade-Giles system. As either systems can be used, this can lead to confusion.

Translating from one language to another can cause difficulties. For example when a German speaker says 'you *must*', he means 'you *should*'; but one can see what problems arise if the German version is translated into Italian when this changes into 'you have to'.

When in the context of a car advertisement the phrase 'body by Brown' was translated literally it read 'corpse by Brown' and the motto 'Let Hertz put you in the driver's seat' was translated into Spanish as 'Let Hertz make you a chauffeur'.

There is the story of an instruction leaflet, written in Italian, for a Microsoft Mouse assembled in Taiwan, which described the product as a 'Micro-tender Rat'.

One also hears of an Emergency Exit at an airport in China which displayed a sign in English stating: 'No entry at peacetime'.

Another classic blunder took place at an international event. A very senior British government official or civil servant with the official title of 'permanent under-secretary' was described in a translated document as an 'immortal typist' whilst in another document he was described as an 'everlasting typist'.

Also read

- Business correspondence
- Jokes and anecdotes
- Language
- Verbal and visual presentations

Intra-National and Intra-Regional Differences

It is quite a common practice to generalise about countries and to stereotype their inhabitants, be they one of the larger nations such as the United States of America and Russia or one of the smaller ones like Belgium. While undoubtedly there are many national traits, there are also within every country, communities, groups, social classes, and other community subsets and minorities who might include those of different religious or ethnic or political persuasions those who are different and often quite distinct from the generally perceived stereotypes national image or so-called norm. These differences might be reflected in many features including language or dialect, food and drink consumption patterns, work ethics and social interactions.

These regional or local differences apply not only to historic nationality groups such as the Scots, the Welsh and the Northern Irish in the British Isles, the Andalucians and the Basques in Spain, the Flemish, the Walloons and German-speaking minority in Belgium and the Bavarians and Swabians in Germany. They are also applicable to the many racial and ethnic groupings in the United States of America. Often, when asked, persons from such communities or groups initially declare themselves as belonging to their particular community or group and only afterwards as being a national of a particular country.

Very often these nationality groups are the victims of jokes. There is the story about the Irish which, it is stated, had been published in *The Irish Times*. 'Water restrictions have been imposed in some parts of the country because of drought. We cannot confirm the story, however, that a notice has been displayed in a swimming pool in the South West saying: Because of water shortage, lanes one, two, seven and eight have been closed.'

Also read

- Ethnic stereotyping

JOKES AND ANECDOTES

It is a mistake to assume that a simple joke or an amusing anecdote can be easily and effectively translated, even by highly skilled interpreters. Jokes about ethnic minorities in one's own country are seldom understood in another country, although practically every country has ethnic or other form of minorities who are their usual targets of ridicule.

The following is allegedly a true story. At a gathering of journalists from various countries it was decided to stage a contest to write about elephants. The consequent article headlines were:

By the American — How to breed a bigger and better elephants;
by the French — The love life of African elephants;
by the Italian — Hannibal, elephants and the fantastic Brenner Pass;
by the Spaniard — Techniques of elephant baiting and fighting;
by the British — How I shot my first elephant in Central Africa;
by the Russian — How we sent an elephant to the moon;
by the Swedish — elephants and the welfare state;
by the German — The cultural and sociological factors relating to elephants, in particular their description in the archives of primitive tribes;
by the Austrians — An elephant's recollections of the old Opera House in Vienna.

If one retains the services of an interpreter, a really good one will let one know when the person with whom one is in conversation has made a joke, as did Honey in the American Doonesbury cartoon series, when she told the audience: 'The joke has been made. He will be expecting you to laugh at it. Go wild!'

Equally difficult to translate are idioms, phrases, proverbs and poems. The story is told of the English phrase 'out of sight out of mind' being translated into Thai as 'invisible things are insane', and the phrase 'the spirit is willing but the flesh is weak' being translated as 'the liquor is holding out all right, but the meat has spoiled'.

Also read

- Interpreting and translating
- Language
- Sense of humour, laughter and smiles

LANGUAGE

Learning a language is no substitute for learning the culture and correct behaviour. One should bear in mind that there are something like 4,000 languages which are spoken by the world's 6.65 billion population (2008 estimate). People who are fluent in a second language but who are not sensitive to the culture of that particular country can sometimes create an even worse impression, than someone who does not speak their language, perhaps because people living in that particular foreign country expect more from someone who speaks their language. Language also includes aspects such as intonation, pitch, melody, and pace or tempo of speech. It is therefore not only what one says, but how one says it. When speaking a foreign language one may unconsciously transmit a false impression, for example curtness in speech, timing of verbal exchanges including periods of silence in a conversation or negotiation, which can lead to misinterpretations.

Language is the most obvious difference between cultures since it reflects its nature and values. The English language for example has a richer vocabulary for commercial and industrial activities than other languages, while others are richer in those subjects that are important to their culture. The Arabic language, for example, is far more than a vehicle for communication and those not acquainted with it are often surprised by the florid nature of Arabic conversation. It not merely expresses ideas but also creates a mood.

There are languages that are tonal, as for example Chinese and Thai, in which each word has not only its sound as indicated by its spelling but also a difference in the pitch at which a particular syllable is pronounced which then determines its meaning. Misunderstanding can easily arise if appropriate sounds are articulated incorrectly.

Even where the language used is almost identical, such as English as spoken in North America or in the United Kingdom, Spanish as spoken in South American countries or in Spain, French as in France or in Canada, there are marked differences in words and expressions that are used as well as in their pronunciation and writing.

There is also the ever present risk of mishearing not only in one's mother tongue but even in a foreign language in which one is reasonably competent. In English the word for a misheard phrase or sentence is a 'mondegreen'. It is based on a Scottish ballad *The Bonny Earl of Murray* which includes the words:

'They ha'e slain the Earls of Murray
And Lady Mondegreen'
however the precise words are:
'They ha'e slain the Earls of Murray
And laid him on the green'

Another and typical example of this is the title of an old English folk dance tune *A Merry Conceit* which many thought was called 'American Seat'.

In addition to mishearing, persons whom one has assumed know a foreign language quite well, can still misinterpret a verbal communication. There is the story of a German travelling on a British ship being asked by a fellow traveller, purely in the course of conversation, whether he was a good sailor replying quite indignantly that he was not a sailor but a consultant.

Speakers of English should be aware that linguists usually divide English speakers into three groups. First, for whom English is the first, and often the only, language. They live in the United Kingdom, the United States of America, Canada, Australia, Jamaica, and other territories of present and former British Empire. Second, those who speak English as their second language. They live in countries where English has a special status either because they were once British colonies or are under strong United States of America influence. They include India, Nigeria, Singapore, The Philippines. The third group — the growing number of people learning English as a foreign language in countries with no strong connection with the United Kingdom or the United States of America.

Language problems occur in some of the second and third group of countries when words are used which have slowly developed in these countries, but are not recognised nor understood by those in the first group of countries, that is by those whose first language is English. The South African English dictionary, for example, contains in the region of 10,000 words that are not used anywhere else.

One should be aware that British English as spoken in the United Kingdom is normally spoken at around 200 words per minute, newsreaders and auctioneers however may speak faster, whilst air traffic controllers, slower. Research suggests that French, Spanish and Italian sounds faster to English speakers, and that Arabic and Russian do not. These perceptions should be borne in mind when speaking in English with persons whose English is not their first language.

There are languages, such as Thai, where a more refined form is spoken among the higher socio-economic classes, as distinct from the language of servants and others further down the social scale. In Japan the language of men differs in a number of respects from that used by women. In many countries several versions of the same basic language may be used in parallel, for example the so-called normal language as used by the middle class, that which is used by the working class, and slang used by groups such as students.

Some languages, for instance Turkish and Hungarian are totally gender-neutral, even using the same word for 'he' and 'she'.

Other languages, for example, English, Arabic and Hebrew are totally gender-inflected.

The vocabulary of a language reflects the culture of its people. Sometimes there are ideas, concepts and words which do not exist in other cultures, they may be technological terminology, concepts in economics and business and even related to sport. It is therefore essential in order not to talk past each other, and to find out what they do mean, in order to prevent misunderstandings. In some Arabic speaking countries, the camel, has been and still is of great economic importance and this is reflected in their language which contains more than 6,000 words for the camel, its parts and its equipment. The English language has an huge vocabulary covering industry, commerce, automotive transport and electronic communication. The Eskimos and those living in very cold climates have a large number of words for describing and classifying snow.

Not knowing the nuances of words or being careless with intonation, might make one say something that one did not mean to say. In many languages there are words that have vulgar or offensive meanings if pronounced incorrectly. The French sometimes speak about 'faux amis' or 'false friends' when referring to words which have similar sounds or give similar verbal impressions but mean something different. The French expression 'nous demandons' does not translate into English as 'we demand' but 'we request'. Similarly the word 'Chef' which in German means a head of a unit, or boss, or chief, while in English it usually means a superior cook in a restaurant.

The language recognised for use in the official domain for instance as used in courts of law and public documents is usually referred to as the official language. It is usually also the language of instruction and teaching. There are many countries which are pluri-lingual and these countries have more than one official language for both governmental and business purposes. The Indian Constitution for example recognises 15 official languages, in addition to English, and these use 11 different scripts. There are countries where one may find many other non-official, informal and local languages or dialects which are in use. There may be a lingua franca or a common language used as means of communication among groups of people whose mother tongues differ.

In some countries people have very strong emotional feelings in respect of their own language or mother tongue, particularly where the language of the, often former colonising power sometimes referred to as 'the imperialism of language' was imposed and their own language treated as inferior. It can however lead to misunderstandings and there have been instances where well-meaning foreign employers spoke to their local employees in their mother tongue. This led to considerable upset because they thought they were being spoken to in their mother tongue because the foreigner considered them unintelligent and unable to converse in the official language or the language of the former colonial power. As can be seen, this can be a delicate or touchy subject in which, whatever one tries to do, one could find oneself in a no-win situation.

There are a number of countries where there may be more than one way of writing their language. In the former Yugoslavia, for example, Serbo-Croat was the main and most important language and while in Belgrade, then in the province of Serbia it was printed in Cyrillic script, while in Zagreb then in the province of Croatia the romanised script was used. One would therefore have need of two script versions when advertising in that country.

In practically every language and culture there are words which should neither be spoken or written. Many revolve around sex and sexual orientation. Some may be blasphemous in that they show disrespect to a religion or something held sacred, they could include curses or swear words, or a profane oath. While some such words and expressions will be considered offensive, insulting or rude there are others which may well be taboo. A language is however a living thing and the meaning of words do change. Even in this day and age, authorities in some countries occasionally still pass laws banning the use of some words, although they may be in common use.

Individual words too can have relatively different meanings in different cultures depending upon expectations, values and experience of the two persons, the speaker and the listener. For example a word such as 'far' when applied to distance, may convey something totally different to a city dweller in North America who practically never walks anywhere, compared with someone who lives on the land in the middle of an African country. Similarly words such as 'big' or 'large' when related to size of an object or a contract.

In the various languages, punctuation marks and other symbols such as the full stop (.), the comma (,) the colon (:), the semicolon (;), the question mark (?), the quotation mark (') and many others are not necessarily written in the same way, nor positioned in the same manner within text. Many different kinds of diacritical signs and marks are used, and some specialist signs and ligatures, such as the ampersand (&) or the 'at' sign (@) may not be understood.

All languages using romanised script are written from left to right on a horizontal line, while many others including Arabic script and languages in Asia and South East Asia are written from right to left. Chinese characters, pictographs or ideograms are printed from top to bottom in vertical columns shifting from right to left, but sometimes also from left to right in horizontal lines.

There is a saying in diplomatic circles, that when a diplomat says yes, he means maybe; if he says maybe he means no; and if he says no, he is no diplomat. It is to oversimplify matters to state that in Western European countries and in North America the word 'yes' means the affirmative and 'no' the negative, in many other countries and cultures even these two words are often the cause of serious misunderstandings. In France people will often say 'no', when they actually mean — maybe, but try and convince me.

In most European languages the response to a question is 'yes' or 'no' according to whether the answer is positive or negative, as in the following examples:

Question	Answer to be conveyed	Answer
1. Is your name Peter?	(My name is Peter)	Yes
2. Is your name Peter?	(My name is **not** Peter)	No
3. Isn't your name Peter?	(My name is Peter)	Yes
4. Isn't your name Peter?	(My name is **not** Peter)	No

But in many African and other languages the choice of 'yes' or 'no' is made in the light of whether the question and answer are both negative, when the answer is 'yes', but if they are not, it will be,'no'. The answers to the four questions above are therefore:

1. Affirmative question + affirmative answer = Yes
2. Affirmative question + negative answer = No
3. Negative question + affirmative answer = No
4. Negative question + negative answer = Yes

A typical example could be the reply to a negative question, such as 'You have no underground railway in this town?' The reply in many African countries might well be: 'Yes, we have none.'

During conversations, discussions and even negotiations with people who live in Asian countries one will notice that they seldom say no. This is not, because there may not be an equivalent word in their language but because they wish to save face or embarrassment for both parties. Instead they may use euphemism or vague, neutral or indirect words and phrases rather than a direct or unforgiving — no.

It should also be noted that in many cultures people will tell you what they think you would want and like to hear, even by the way of giving you directions. They may use words such as 'not far', when the destination may well be a long way away.

Often the answer to a language problem is the need to read 'between the lines'. This indicates that one has to analyse what has not been said rather than what has been said.

In some languages such as German and most of the Scandinavian languages the information conveyed by the language is explicit and words have specific meaning, while in others such as Arabic and Japanese it is not necessarily so.

There are sometimes hidden or subtle meanings in words and expressions which are not obvious to foreigners even if they have a good knowledge of a language. There is the story of a tired businessman telephoning the reception desk in a hotel in a country in the Middle East requesting 'an extra pillow', and to his surprise immediately being sent up a girl. If he made a similar request in a British hotel he might well be asked, whether he would like the pillow to be feather or foam filled.

There are basically two types of languages. There are the dead languages such as Ancient Greek, Latin and Sanskrit which are learned for historical or religious reasons without being part of everyday linguist exchange and living languages currently in use worldwide. Because languages in current use are alive, they are the method of conveying new ideas, innovations and concepts. There is therefore a constant stream of new words which enter languages, as well as changes in the interpretation of existing words. This too can cause of misunderstandings, even when people talk the same language and even the use of identical words could mean different things. Changes take place more rapidly in the context of the spoken language than when it is written. The compilers of the Oxford English Dictionary, for example, state that around 1,000 new words, worth recording, are added to the English language every year.

Sign language is a central part of the deaf culture. There is no universal sign language and every country, with a few exceptions, has its own form of sign language, for example:

ASL — American Sign Language
LSF — Langue des Signes Française
DGS — German Sign Language
BSL — British Sign Language

Just as there are within countries regional forms of speech, pronunciation and accents so there are regional differences in sign language. Attempts have been made to try to create an international sign language and there is a little know sign language called 'International Sign' Pidgin, however, its lexicon or vocabulary is still quite limited.

Braille is a system of embossed type used by the blind and by partially sighted persons for reading and writing. It is also used by them for recreational activities such as playing chess. Most written languages have a set of Braille symbols representing that language. Each language creates its own sets of rules concerning those symbols. Related means of communication for the blind and partially sighted are 'talking products and goods', such as talking books, newspapers and other items for daily living and recreational purposes.

Also read

- Conversation and communication
- Courtesy
- Email, netiquette and cyberspace behaviour
- Interpreting and translating
- Jokes and anecdotes
- Verbal and visual presentations

Laws and Legal Systems

One interpretation of 'law' in its widest meaning is that it comprises all rules of conduct established by the governing authorities, as well as established customs of a community. The term, legal systems is usually used when one mentions the system of courts and tribunals within which such rules are applied in the course of the administration of justice. By this is meant administration of justice in accordance with law and not merely the abstract concept.

Legal systems and laws vary from country to country, some are entirely civil in nature, others are based to varying degrees on religion. The former are practised in most Western culture countries, while the latter includes the Islamic view, which is based on the concept that the first law for man to obey is the law of God and not the law of the State, and the provisions of the Shariah, therefore, combines the moral, religious and judicial laws.

The assertion that all men are equal under the law does not apply worldwide and in some countries the law may well be applied and interpreted differently depending on the sex, socio-economic level, political persuasion, connections or the racial, religious or ethnic background of those bringing or defending accusations. Access to the law, that is the ability to enforce legal rights or defend oneself may also not be readily available, everywhere. Legal proceedings are expensive and systems of legal aid, if available, varies considerably from country to country.

Laws are created either through legislation by the executive or by the legislature and this system is known as statute or statutory law alternatively, they are established by cases in law courts which then provides a system of precedents and this is known as common or case law.

Statute law takes the form of broad statements of overriding principles and aims and effect is given to these by a hierarchy of more specific rules, each level being read subject to the superior principles. Under case law greater emphasis is placed on the wording of the law and on previous court rulings and judgements.

There is a substantial difference between procedures under statute law and procedures under common law. In the former, the court procedures tend to be an enquiry into the truth by the judge, who plays an active part in the proceedings. Under the common law system the procedure tends to be adversarial, that is the opposing lawyers or counsels make the best case possible for their clients with the judge, as a kind of referee, finally making the decision or if a there is a jury, highlighting the issues for which their decision is required.

Other differences in legal systems include relative power in the hands of judges compared with juries, and what is and is not admitted as evidence, fact, hearsay and gossip.

Branches of the law with which business executives and officials could be involved might be administrative law and criminal law. Other sectors include the laws of contract — the concept of offer and acceptance, the contents of contracts, remedies for breach of contract and non-performance. The law of property includes distinctions between ownership and possession and its legal effects, sale, lease, hiring and related transactions.

In connection with business, be it industry or commerce, laws regulate the setting up of a business, whether as a sole trader, a partnership or a limited company, commercial contracts with suppliers and customers both in the domestic or home market and in foreign markets, including those relating to manufacture, distribution, and licensing or franchising. In the context of business, assets may not only refer to property such as factories, warehouses, shops and the like but also to copyright, trade marks, patents and know-how. There are laws relating to acquisition of companies, their disposal and reconstruction. Other branches of the law cover activities relating to exports and imports. There is also employment law, with its subdivisions relating to race, sex and age discrimination, employment protection, pension schemes and the like.

Laws relating to financing of business in all forms as well as the organisations and persons providing financial services are governed by a wide range of diverse systems of regulatory legislation in practically every country. There is the subject of environmental law to which industry and commerce are subject, including planning rules and regulations.

Many hundreds of people are arrested every year when they visit foreign countries for actual or alleged transgression of national or local laws, rules and regulations. Such arrests may be related to perceived violations of regulations — governing the import or export of goods including smuggling, business fraud, illegal currency transactions, drunken and disorderly behaviour, offending religious rules, customs and taboos, taking unauthorised photographs, being in prohibited areas, motor vehicle-related offences, not complying with regulation governing crossing a road on foot, those relating to drugs and many others. It is advisable to be aware of relevant laws and regulations, particularly if engaged in commerce or trade since *ignorance of the law is usually no defence.*

Because of different national laws and regulations applicable to banking and credit problems can be encountered by visitors to other countries. In some countries it is a criminal offence to have a cheque stopped because the Bank did not honour the cheque. A similar attitude may be taken by the authorities to payments made with credit cards, if the credit limit has been exceeded.

In Europe there is an additional legal system — the Law of the European Union. This operates alongside the laws of the individual member states of the European Union. In many spheres the Law of the European Union takes priority over national law of individual European Community member states.

In some countries it may be difficult to establish what the law says on a specific matter because there may not be any laws or legal codes covering the subject.

One should also be aware that there are countries where there are few if any procedures for issues such as protesting bills, debt collection and arbitration, for company law including bankruptcy and liquidation, for laws concerning offences arising out of ownership of motor vehicles including accidents and personal injuries, immigration, employment and labour laws, intellectual property legislation including patents, trade marks and copyright. Then again where such procedures do exist they may differ significantly from those in one's own country. There are countries where there are no laws governing agency legislation, which may instead be regulated by traditional national commercial and business practices.

Cultural differences and legal orientation in other countries and other business cultures can and do account for differences in the meaning and interpretation of legal phrases, idioms and expressions and often more suitable and more appropriate alternatives will have to be found. For example, the term 'force majeure' in some countries has a particular meaning, in others it will only be possible to establish a clear meaning if the parties concerned define it for themselves in their agreement.

In many Western culture countries the legal term *Act of God* is usually used for events outside human control. However for a number of reasons including those based on religion, this turn of phrase may be unacceptable in some countries and other expressions, such as 'conditions beyond the control of the parties' may have to be used.

During an international conference on Maritime matters it was realised that the languages used in some countries do not contain the expression 'Maritime fraud', their only equivalent being piracy, which in most countries is a very different type of crime or offence.

When an agreement to a transaction has been reached, whether or not there is some formalisation or contract and how it is to be interpreted is very much culture related. Parties to an agreement may consider that relationships, tradition, religion and culture are better protection against breach of contract than the law. While people from some countries, for example those in western Europe and North America, will not conclude business without some form of a written contract, others may consider that a person's word is more binding than a written agreement and consider insistence on a written contract as an insult.

In many countries there are alternative ways and means of settling commercial disputes, since court proceedings are both time consuming and cost a lot of money. These methods of resolving disputes include: arbitration and mediation. In Japan, the lawyer is normally called in only when problems have reached a crisis stage. One should try to remember an old Asian saying: 'When a lawyer shows up, it is like the appearance of a Buddhist priest who is called in to administer the last rites'.

The way the legal profession is organised or structured is often very dissimilar in different countries and this can have considerable implications and effects on the way in which lawyers function. This also has implications in regard the rules and laws relating to them. For example, in some countries the concept of 'professional privilege' applies to communications between the lawyer and his client so that the lawyer cannot be required to disclose what passed between him and his client in connection with the lawsuit. In other countries this concept may not apply with the same intensity nor scope. This concept of confidentiality may on occasions also apply to specific exchanges of communication between opposing lawyers.

One should be aware that the phrase 'without prejudice' which is used in the course of negotiations in common law in the United Kingdom is not known in most countries, except a few that are those that once were part of the British Empire. This legal phrase allows parties, either a person or a group of people acting together, to discuss and negotiate a settlement to a legal claim, without admitting liability. Any documents headed 'without prejudice' cannot be used in evidence in any subsequent court case without the permission of both parties.

Also read

- Censorship
- Negotiating and bargaining
- Travelling

LEISURE AND LEISURE ACTIVITIES

Among executives and officials in different countries the relationship between work and leisure tends to be quite dissimilar.

While the culture of some countries stresses benefits of a virtuous or balanced personal life as being more important than personal achievement or profit, in other countries and cultures the notion 'success at any cost' applies, even if it is perhaps not the norm.

Many senior executives in Western culture countries provide an extreme example of this and often use leisure as an extension of work. If they have any leisure time it is infused by considerations relating to their work, which represents their dominant interest in life. It then becomes increasingly difficult to draw any line between their work and their leisure activities.

An article in an American golf magazine stated that golf has transcended the parameters of simply being a sport. It went on the say that golf courses had become an extension of the boardroom. It continued, that it was a gold mine of business contacts as almost all American executives play a round of golf every once a while. It suggested that golf brought golf playing persons closer to another as there was more time for discussion and interaction than at business meetings. Furthermore that it provided an opportunity to see another and different side of the other person, other than one seen in a boardroom or at business meetings.

Also read

- Business entertaining
- The way of life, lifestyle or quality of life

LINKS AND CONNECTIONS

The usefulness of having connections in business depends very much on the business culture of the country concerned. In countries where it requires considerable expertise on how to conduct business taking into account complex local bureaucracy, particularly in dealings with the governmental sector, an intermediary or facilitator is invaluable. In some countries it is vital to have a go-between or intermediary to assist with opening doors, in others while perhaps not essential, it is still most useful.

There are many countries where ties based on wealth, education, family or other factors make up a strong 'old boy network'. This applies both in the commercial and the governmental sectors. A business visitor without introductions can waste much time and effort to achieve a breakthrough. As a generalisation a well-connected visitor is more likely to be successful in being granted an appointment or interview without too much delay, than a person without an introduction. The old precept 'it doesn't matter what you know, but who you know', is still as relevant today as it has ever been.

A well-known expression for connections is the term 'networking', while in Spain the term 'enchufado' is used for a well-connected person, it is derived from the word 'enchufe' or electric plug, because the person, whom one could describe as a facilitator brings about introductions and thereby causes the current to flow.

What one should be aware of is that in some countries requesting an introduction or receiving a recommendation via a facilitator is the equivalent of establishing an obligation, which in turn might well lead to a future counter-request.

It depends very much on the country one intends to visit as to which kind of intermediary is likely to be the most useful. It could be anyone of the following: the company's local agent, the company's bank and accountants, a chamber of commerce, trade and industry or the commercial section of one's embassy. There are many other channels which should be considered including: editors of trade magazines, international associations of one's professional or trade association, one's clubs and sports clubs, international links of organisations such as Freemasons, Rotary and Lions Clubs.

Also read

- Social contact

Losing and Saving Face

The concept of *face* relates to any encounter where someone's credibility has been challenged during a personal exchange in a given situation. *Face* can be interpreted as any of the following: honour, good reputation, dignity, prestige or respect. Although in general the Asian concept of face is similar to that as understood in Western culture countries, it is far more important. Causing someone to lose face in Asian countries, even if the offence was unintended could cause serious damage to a relationship.

Saving face is sometimes described as making a point without winning an argument, meaning that the other party need not *lose face*. While in Western culture countries this is often interpreted as applying only to an individual, in many Asian countries it can relate to a group, which may be the family or the company of which the individual is a part. A person who is embarrassed in public in such a manner that others become aware of it, shares that embarrassment with his group. Saving face is aimed at maintaining harmonious relations.

In most Western culture societies anger can be expressed loudly and vociferously and usually no harm is done. In many Asian and South East Asian countries similar behaviour is considered inexcusable and persons who act in such a manner will suffer loss of face as well as loss of respect which they may have great difficulty to regain.

Actions designed to save face can result in behaviour that can easily be misinterpreted by someone who does not understand this concept. If a subordinate argues or disagrees with a superior in a business organisation, the superior would lose face. This helps to explain why an Asian employee might publicly agree with his Western culture employer while privately continuing to do things his own way. A result of this could be that Western culture person might consider that this behaviour to be dishonest while an Asian person would think this is polite. Another feature of this cultural characteristic is that people may avoid being critical when an incisive comment might well be more appropriate.

A European executive based in Hong Kong commented that it is possible to lose face if he telephoned a Chinese businessman to arrange a meeting. He stated that it implied that you have no one to do it for you, nor did it give the Chinese businessman the opportunity to say no, without causing offence.

There is an account of a foreign lecturer in a school in South East Asian country who was giving a lesson. Suddenly, during the lesson a rat fell on his desk. He immediately hit and killed it. His students told him that he would receive a reward if he took the dead rat to the Rat Collection Bureau. What the lecturer did not know was that neither the Bureau nor the school wanted to lose face. The Bureau therefore refused to pay the lecturer on the basis that he was a foreigner. The school denied that there was a rat problem and paying the lecturer a reward would be an admission that there was a rat problem. This incident is an indication just how far some people in some cultures will go in order not to lose face by admitting fault.

Also read

- Business ideology, management style and decision making
- Manners, conduct and behaviour
- Negotiating and bargaining

MALE-FEMALE RELATIONSHIPS

Most societies have conventions concerning public display of affection between sexes, as well as restrictions attached to tactile relationships, particularly with the opposite sex. While in some societies it is socially perfectly acceptable for men to walk with their arm on another man's shoulder or holding hands, or for girls and women to hold each others' hands, in a number of countries in the Middle East it would not be permitted for men and women to touch each other in public.

This aspect of local culture was overlooked when an international entertainment company decided to stage a spectacular Italian opera outdoors in Upper Egypt. In the tradition of this Western style opera in some of the scenes men and women danced together. Since this is not a custom permitted in some of the Islamic countries it was not approved by the local authorities, and at the last minute, in order not to cancel the event, the producer had to re-choreograph several acts and was involved in considerable additional expenditure in engaging additional male dancers.

When the Warner-Lambert Company used its American advertisement for mouthwash showing a boy and girl being affectionate to each other, it was not an effective promotional aid in Thailand since the boy-girl relationship shown was considered to be ultra-modern and not in keeping with the cultural traditions of the country. Sales improved, when the advertisement was subsequently modified to show two girls talking to each other.

In nearly all Western style countries it is customary for men and women to greet each other by shaking hands. Only in a few Western style countries is *corporate* kissing between men and women practised and then only among old acquaintances. However, when men try to greet business women whom they hardly know by kissing their cheek instead of a handshake, this can offend women's susceptibilities since they may well consider such physical contact patronising by conveying an impression that a woman should be treated differently to a man in an otherwise normal business relationship. Women executives sometimes commit similar faux pas when greeting businessmen.

Office romances are often an inevitable part of working life in many countries where members of both sexes are employed. The dividing line between office banter and unwelcome sexual advances can be very fine and cultural factors often determine the position of this dividing line. There are still countries and societies where employers insist that such relationships be avoided. Action taken by employers includes job reassignment or dismissal. Lawsuits arising out of perceived sexual harassment have contributed to greater awareness of this by employers.

In the Middle East and South East Asia there are still a number of countries and within these countries castes, sects and social classes, where a local man would be extremely embarrassed if it was suggested that he should talk with a woman who is not part of his extended family. A man should and must, according to customs and beliefs ignore her, if he wishes to avoid the wrath of her father or her family or her husband.

In some Middle Eastern and Asian countries where it is customary for men shake hands on meeting and parting, the situation is quite different should a man be introduced to a woman. In such situations it would be appropriate to wait to see if the woman offers her hand, before he extends his.

In many countries wearing a ring on a finger is an indication that the man or woman concerned is engaged or married. It should be noted that in some countries a wedding ring is worn on the fourth finger of the left hand, while in others it is customary to wear it on the fourth finger of the right hand. There are a few countries where the wedding ring is worn on a toe instead of a finger. The material used for such rings, as well as the style, design and pattern is very much determined by the customs and traditions of the society of those wearing such rings.

Also read

- Business ideology, management style and decision making
- Greeting, introductions, modes of address and leave-taking
- Religious beliefs
- Sex
- Social kissing
- Women in business and the professions

MANNERS, CONDUCT AND BEHAVIOUR

When visiting any foreign country it is essential to realise that social conventions and protocol might be more liberal or alternatively more puritanical or perhaps just basically different from those which apply in one's own country. They might, for example, include unusual conventions regarding meeting and greeting of persons and expressions of gratitude, deference and respect towards one's elders, attitude vis-à-vis members of the opposite sex, attitude towards those of similar and those of different status and appropriate ways of entering the offices of other people.

It includes ways of laughing, where in some countries such as Japan a person might cover his mouth with one hand indicating that he is not laughing at someone. Also under the heading of manners are other acts which might be described as ordinary or basic body functions, where some acts which might be considered polite in one society might be interpreted as bad manners in another, these could include yawning, coughing, sneezing or blowing one's nose.

There are many countries where particular institutions or persons are held in great respect and reverence. These could, for example, include the royal family or the clergy and it would not be advisable to speak about them disrespectfully. Similarly signs of respect are sometimes extended to include national memorials, images, statues even postage stamps. In Thailand the king and his family are treated with great reverence and should never be insulted or criticised. Those who have been prosecuted by the authorities include a Swiss man who sprayed graffiti on the king's portrait and a Greek-Australian writer for allegedly insulting the royal family. Advice for those visiting includes to comment, that should a coin or note drop on the floor, not to touch money with one's foot, because all currency has the king's likeness on it, and touching with one's foot amounts to kicking the king on the head.

There are societies, in Asia and particularly in South East Asia, where to show in public being angry or upset is equated with losing face and a serious flaw of character. This is very different from some Western societies where some public displays of feeling, for example being angry, may sometimes be used as a negotiating ploy.

One should be aware that persons who show some understanding of local conduct and behaviour are bound to create a more favourable impression with their hosts.

Also read

- Body language and non-verbal communication
- Conversation and communication
- Etiquette, customs and conventions
- Losing face and saving face

MEASURING AND MANAGING TIME

In most, but not all countries the Gregorian calendar, based on 365 days and 366 days in a leap-year, is used. The year is divided into 12 months, and into weeks of seven days. Other units of time are expressed in hours, minutes and seconds. This is not a universal system and many other forms of calendars are in existence. When other systems are in operation the figures used to indicate the year are usually sufficiently different for this to be obvious.

In some calendars, a year may also be divided into units other than 12 months. In Ethiopia the year is divided into 12 months of 30 days each and one month of five days, or six days every fourth (leap) year.

In many countries, including Afghanistan, China, India, Iran, Israel, Japan, Myanmar, Sri Lanka and Thailand a lunar based calendar systems are used, usually concurrently with the Western culture or Gregorian calendar. It is important to be aware that this may have a bearing on the calendar dates when national secular and religious holidays are celebrated. It may also have an effect on the starting date of the governmental fiscal or taxation year.

The two main international timekeeping conventions are the 12 hour clock system and 24 hour clock system. Most countries operate under one of these two systems, there are also a few that use both systems at the same time. The British am (morning) and pm (afternoon) convention is not known nor used in many countries. Most of those countries using the 12 hour clock system have a turn of phrase to differentiate between morning hours and afternoon or evening hours, for example between 6 o'clock in morning and 6 o'clock in the afternoon.

One should also be aware that some countries covering a huge area of land, for instance Russia and the United States, are divided into a large number of time zones between their eastern and western borders.

A large number of countries operate daylight savings time adjustments. Its commencement, duration and ending is usually determined by national regulations. A few countries permit some of their states or regions to opt out of national regulations, resulting in more than one time zone.

What is more confusing is when different systems of time are used; although in most countries the *clock time* is used as a means of measuring time, there are some countries or regions where a system that might be titled *event-time* is used to measure time.

In an event-time system, time is related to events. This might be an historic event such as an earthquake or wedding of the head of state, alternatively a daily routine event like morning prayers.

Even in the clock time method there are different systems, in country districts in Ethiopia for example, sunrise is always zero hour and therefore 07.00 hours or 7 am is 1 o'clock. Similarly in Thailand, when not using the 24 hour system, Thais divide the day into four sections of six hours and to meet someone at 'four in the morning' is quite likely to mean at 10.00 hours.

The expression used for a particular point in time varies from country to country, and it is not uncommon for such indications of time to be mistranslated or misunderstood, thus *noon* which means 12 o'clock midday in some countries may mean 14.00 hours or 2 pm or 2 o'clock in others. The German expression 'halb neun' or 'half nine' means 08.30 hours and not 09.30 hours.

In Malaysia, if a guest is invited to a house on Saturday at 19.30 hours, this really means that one should come on Friday evening at 19.30 hours, since Malays consider that the new day really starts at about 18.30 hours. One would therefore be well advised to establish, in good time, with one's host the precise date and time of the invitation so as to avoid making a mistake by arriving on the wrong day. Likewise it is essential to carefully check date and time with one's host in Indonesia where the day begins at sunset and the night of a day *precedes* the day rather than following it.

Also read

- Appointments
- Punctuality, duration and terminating a business visit
- Sense of time
- Units of measure

MUSIC AND SOUND

Music, whether it is a rhythmic sequence of pleasing sounds, a chant, a melody or any other form of expressive composition, very often has strong and usually a special and obvious relationship with the culture of a country or a society. It could be a national anthem, a folk song, a traditional dance, a religious hymn, a television or radio jingle or a tune used by supporters of a football or sports team. It has been said that every sound has a special meaning in every culture.

There are various customs and conventions associated with the playing of National Anthems in almost every country. One should be aware of these if invited to attend official or formal functions when the National Anthem is being played at indoor or outdoor events. Such conventions might well include whether to stand or remain seated and whether or not to remove one's hat or head-dress.

Occasionally when there have been fundamental government changes, for instance a revolution or a military coup, playing the former anthem may be forbidden and replaced with a new anthem. In other cases the music of the anthem may be retained but new words substituted. There have been occasions, for instance sporting events between national teams, when due to unawareness or oversight a banned anthem has been played. While this has sometimes had only limited consequences it has at times led to disturbances inside and outside sports arenas and resulted in harmful relationships between nations. A case in point was the tennis Davis Cup Finals in Australia in 2003. Spanish players and official were greatly upset when the trumpeter played the pre-civil war Spanish Republican anthem which had been provided in error to the event organiser.

Because in many countries some music may well have religious, ceremonial and even a political significance, the choice of music for advertising or promotional purposes requires careful consideration. Music from one culture may not only be unfamiliar to those belonging to another but may also be found distasteful or perhaps offensive. Similar reactions could be relevant to music used in television and radio programmes, in films, video or any other kind of electronic transmissions via the Internet.

Also read

- Advertising
- Aesthetics or appreciation of beauty

NAMES

It is sometimes said that 'a person's name to them is the sweetest and most important sound in any language'.

Usually the problem when a name is translated within those languages that use the romanised script is that of pronunciation.

A whole range of different problems arise when personal and family names are translated between languages using different alphabets and/or different scripts. Many countries and cultures practice a wide range of procedures and conventions to deal with this including romanisation of names and matters concerning sequence of names, for example given name first, followed by the family name. Other problems arise when a name is translated, or transposed or transliterated, perhaps using an onomatopoeic convention, since the newly translated or transposed name could inadvertently mean something unlucky or disagreeable.

A Japanese visitor to Tanzania encountered considerable embarrassment since, when his name was transposed into Kiswahili, it was the same as the local slang for the male genetalia.

As there is no typical alphabet in the Chinese language it uses characters that all mean something. People wishing to do business in China convert their name into Chinese use characters that either sound vaguely like their family name or have a impressive meaning. This can however create problems. During his earlier career a British governor-general in Hong Kong had chosen three characters in Mandarin Chinese which were pronounced Wei De-wei. When he moved to Hong Kong, where Chinese is spoken in the Cantonese Chinese dialect, the pronunciation of these characters was Ngai Tak-ngai. In Cantonese the first Ngai can mean false or counterfeit, and the second Ngai suggested a traditional unlucky tale which is an omen of extreme bad luck. Altogether it had most unfitting and unsuitable connotation. He therefore chose a new Chinese name Wai Yik-shun which in the local, Cantonese, dialect suggests — full of confidence and great faith.

Chinese people often inspect a visitors business card to see if the Chinese name has a propitious meaning. A good name can bring all manner of good luck, an inauspicious name the opposite.

In Myanmar people do not have a family name. There a woman retains her own name even after marriage. The basis for naming a child is usually the day of the week on which it was born.

The name of persons in Korea has two parts, a family name and a given name. As there are only around 250 family or clan names, this creates problems. To overcome such problems they use titles connected with their profession, place of work and rank. Women retain their names when they marry, but children take their father's name. Koreans romanise their name in various ways. Some adhere to the original order or sequence of names, that is family name followed by given name, while others reverse them to match Western culture patters.

The story is told of the British journalist Horatio Bottomley arriving at the home of Lord Cholmondley. He said to the butler 'I wish to speak to Lord Cholmondley'.

'Lord Chumley, sir,' the butler replied, correcting his pronunciation.

'Oh, all right,' said Horatio Bottomley. 'Tell him that 'Mr. Bumley' would like to see him.'

Also read

- Business cards
- Forms of address and use of titles
- Greeting, introductions, modes of address and leave-taking
- Telephoning
- Women in business and the professions

NATIONAL AND PUBLIC HOLIDAYS AND FESTIVALS BOTH SECULAR AND RELIGIOUS

In most countries, the date of practically all secular public holidays are based on custom and tradition, and fixed in advance. There are however some countries where the dates of some of secular public holidays are only announced during the previous year. In the case of religious holidays and festivals, while many are on fixed dates, others are dependent on the lunar calendar and therefore vary from year to year. The commencement of some are even more unpredictable since they are contingent on the sighting of the new moon.

In Muslim countries, during the month of Ramadan, little, if any, business is transacted. During that period it is also forbidden to eat, drink and smoke in public places.

In many Christian countries very little business is transacted during the period between Christmas and the New Year.

Even in relatively smaller countries such as the United Kingdom there are differences between regions such as Scotland and three other regions of the country, England, Wales and Northern Ireland. In Italy each town may have local public holidays on the Feast Day of their particular Patron Saint. In countries with regions with deep-rooted linguistic and cultural traditions, such as for example in Switzerland and in Belgium, each region may observe different religious and secular public holidays in addition to or in place of national holidays.

In several countries, such as in the United States of America, observance of some secular public holidays varies considerably in the different states and territories, since some are established by State legislation.

In some countries, apart from national public holidays, some businesses under the management of persons belonging to large ethnic or religious communities may also close during their particular religious holidays. In the United States, for example, this applies to the garment, fur and jewellery trades in the New York during Jewish religious holidays.

Also read

- Appointments
- Measuring and managing time
- Religious beliefs

NEGOTIATING AND BARGAINING

It is a fact of life that everybody negotiates, but it is only when one negotiates with people from another country, ethnic group or society that it is important to realise that a wide range of cross-cultural factors play an important role.

Safety is one of the elements of negotiating and includes two important elements. *Precaution*, which covers the background and includes knowledge of the foreign culture, and *caution*, which concerns the actual course of bargaining.

Negotiations are usually based on an implicit assumption about the purpose, as well as a range of conventional acumen, beliefs and social expectations. Sometimes the difference between two sides is evident in the basic difference of social behaviour, form and ceremony, prestige and dignity, as well as a preference for subtle versus direct approach. There are, however, many other factors related to the business and cultural environment of the parties concerned, which need to be taken into account.

Included in this are language, body language, using evidence, when and how to raise points, appropriate use of time, speed or pace of the negotiations, decision-making, as well as the position of both parties concerning the honouring of written or oral contracts. Other cultural differences include style of logic and reasoning, as in some cultures people are not convinced by hypothetical reasoning or justification based on principles. Some countries are enthusiastic proponents of compromise, others see less virtue in compromise as such, unless the reasoning is faulty, yet others think that compromise translates into a matter of honour and may feel that something has been lost in the context of values.

In some countries people think of negotiations as a simple bargaining or buying-selling activity that is focused on achieving a specific objective and is concluded when a contract is signed, since this may well be the custom in their own country. There are many countries where this is not the case and in those instances it may be better to consider negotiation activities as steady or ongoing process.

Culture works both visibly and invisibly. Both influence the basis of negotiation and the eventual realisation of the contract. It should also be noted that in some countries relatively long periods of silence in the middle of negotiations are not unusual, and those from Western culture countries are sometimes unsettled by this practice or procedure.

The timing or pace of negotiations is very much culture related. In those industrialised countries, where people subscribe to the guideline that 'time is money', negotiators do not take kindly to delaying tactics. There are however other cultures who subscribe to the view that taking time can be compared with gaining wisdom.

There are times when it is important to break off negotiations either for a temporary recess to review progress, or because no-one is getting anywhere and that a pause may well be needed by either or both sides to rethink positions and strategies.

The process by which people are selected as negotiators varies from country to country; it also depends at what level of seniority the negotiations are being held. Selection at one level may be for technical competence, personal power or authority and on another level it may be based on seniority or social connections. It is therefore advisable to know what role the foreign negotiators in the opposite team might play. When negotiating with people from other countries and cultures it is important to get reliable and in-depth information about the persons whom one is facing across the bargaining table, their biographical details for example, so to be able to be totally aware of their attitudes, their probable strategies and techniques in order to be able to formulate one's own.

When negotiations are conducted with a group or team of people from other countries, it is not necessarily their most senior person who is doing all the talking. There may well be culture related conventions or unwritten rules which determine the role of the various members of the opposite team.

A Thai business person might well react differently to the personal behaviour and its associated mannerism to someone from Germany or to that of a trader from Japan. What would be a normal display of aggressive negotiating in the USA might be interpreted as appalling bad manners in Dubai.

High volume sales through retail outlets such as hypermarkets and supermarkets, particularly in the industrialised countries are not designed for bargaining, as are, for example souks, bazaars and markets in developing countries. This, among other factors, has conditioned some sophisticated consumers in industrialised countries to look down upon those who still bargain daily in shops for food and other items. They forget that they themselves bargain most effectively for every penny, cent or euro-cent, when, for instance, they are buying a house or a car or negotiating their insurance policy.

Throughout many Middle Eastern, Asian and Pacific Region countries bargaining over the price of goods and services is almost an art form. Bargaining as understood by its practitioner is also a method for establishing one's status in an economic community. In the bazaars markets or the souks it is quite probable that one item will have a range of prices each reflecting, in the eye of the seller, the correct price for each of his customers. To offer everyone the same price removes the opportunity to do a favour for his special customer and equally the opportunity to blatantly overcharge an unsuspecting buyer.

In countries where it is the practice in business discussions and negotiations to avoid the direct negative which might imply impoliteness, there are a wide range of conventional phrases, expressions and verbal cues which are used as substitutes for the word 'no'. This means that one should not limit oneself to the literal meaning or word but also analyse the circumstances under which negative and related statements are made. Such statements might contain phrases such as: 'I'll consider it'; 'maybe a little later'; 'we hope we can do that'; 'we wuld like to work that out if we can'; 'problems'; 'perhaps'; 'maybe', or 'it is a little difficult'. For example in Japan one should, also take care not to ask blunt questions in situations where the other party would find it difficult to respond frankly.

Misunderstandings often occur between persons from different cultures and societies in respect of the word 'yes'. When a Western person visits Japan or South Korea for example, his initial reaction, usually based on his own norms, would lead him to expect that a statement like 'yes' to mean 'yes I agree' or some other form of compliance or affirmation, instead the speaker who has just said 'yes' might only have meant to indicate: 'I am listening', or 'I have heard what you say'.

Also read

- Business ideology, management style and decision making
- Language
- Laws and legal systems
- Losing face and saving face

Numbers, Figures and Counting

Around the world there are various methods of writing numbers. In most Western culture countries the Arabic numeral system is used. These are numbers such as 1, 10, 50, 100 which are read from left to right with the highest value on the left, as for example when expressing values such as £312.26, with the 3 representing the highest, and the 6 representing the lowest, or when expressing length — in 15.40m, the 1 refers to the greater value of metres and the 40 the lowest in centimetres. There are many other numbering systems which like the Arabic numeral system are written from right to left. They also position the highest value on the left. The Roman numeric system, such as I, II, III, IV... is often used to number paragraphs in reports and correspondence. One should be aware that Roman style figures might not be understood in every country. In countries where Arabic is the national language the numbering system used is usually Arabic style numerals or figures. Some Arabic-speaking countries refer to this as the Eastern Arabic numeral system. Whilst Arabic is written from right to left, the numbers are written from left to right with the highest value on the left.

In many European countries the number 1 (one) is written in such a style that it can be mistaken for the number 7 (*seven*). Because of this the number 7 usually has a horizontal stroke across its vertical line.

Most countries use a decimal-style numerical scale of 1, 100, 1,000, 100,000 followed by 1,000,000 the equivalent of 1 million or 1 m. Thereafter unfortunately the words used in different become confused and not even the International System of Units (SI) has been able to implement international agreement. A 1 followed by nine zeros or 1,000,000,000 and sometimes written as 19 is variously known as — thousand million, a milliard or a billion, whilst an 1 followed by 12 zeros or 1,000,000,000,000 and sometimes written as 112 is variously known as billion or a trillion. It is therefore advisable to ask for clarification when words such as millions, billions, milliards or trillions are used.

There are also countries where different systems of indicating numbers, and writing multiples of numbers are in use. In India, for example, the units are hundred, thousand, hundred thousand and ten million, and 1 Lakh or 100,000 Rupees is written as 1.00.000 Rupees and 1 Crore, the equivalent of 100 Lakh or 10 million is written 1.00.00.000 Rupees. In Japan there is a unit of 10.000 and larger units such as 1 million are written as 100 x 10.000.

Conventions regarding the separation of groups of figures vary, some countries use a (.) period, full stop, dot or decimal point;

some use a (,) comma, some use a period for separating the whole numbers which are then followed by a comma to separate these from the decimal fractions. In some countries the opposite system is used, yet others use an (') apostrophe to separate the last three digits of a whole number, for example 1.000'000.

Conventions regarding symbols and abbreviations to be used for various currencies, including whether they are to be placed in front of or after the numbers, vary from country to country.

In Spain when the four numbers representing a year are written, a full stop or period (.) is used after the first digit, for example 2.009.

Misunderstandings sometimes arise due to the way in which certain sets of numbers are expressed in the spoken language of a country, for example in the English and the French languages the number 21 is verbally expressed as twenty-one, but in German it is 'ein und zwanzig' or one and twenty.

Certain numbers are credited with being lucky while others are unlucky. In many countries 13 is considered to be unlucky and some hotels avoid having a 13th floor and some airlines do not have a row 13.

In some countries 4 is the unlucky number as, for example, in Japan and Korea where this number when spoken has a somewhat similar sound as the word for death. In some Korean buildings, especially hospitals, there is no 4th floor. Also unlucky in Japan is the number 9 since one meaning of the word for nine is *pain* and the number 49 combining 4 and 9 is considered a particularly unlucky number. There are other countries where figures containing seven, as in 17, 27, 37... are considered more or less unlucky numbers.

Numbers are occasionally endowed with particular meanings. Number 1 is often credited as being first or the best for advertising and promotional purposes, as for example, when combined with the letter A as in A1. In some hotels and public buildings in Austria and some regions of Germany, the door to rooms marked with the numbers 00, denote a toilet or a public convenience.

In Thailand 3 is the lucky number. In Hong Kong the lucky number is 8 and means, 'money is coming'. Combinations of this number, for example 888 used on car number plates and when part of a telephone this number is considered very lucky and much sought after. In Japan too the number 8 is considered lucky.

In Brazil, one of the slang words used to describe a homosexual is synonymous with 'deer', and calling someone by that term is extremely offensive. An illegal lottery 'jogo do bicho' is conducted in that country in which the lottery numbers are assigned an equivalent animal, the number 24 is for the deer group. Since this animal is strongly associated with male homosexuality assigning a man in any way to the number 24 for instance a seat number or a sports jersey would be considered rude, unless this man is a close friend, in which case, it may be considered funny.

Some items and products are traditionally sold in multiples such as batches, sets, aggregates, or groups, these multiples are culturally determined. In many Western culture countries crockery sets such as cups and plates, are usually sold in sets of 6 or 12 pieces, while in Japan a set would consist of 5 or 10 pieces.

Occasionally different counting conventions will be encountered in countries. In the United Kingdom cows or horses will be counted in units of one upwards, but in country districts game birds, for example pheasants, will be counted in units of two and called a brace. In Japan different counting idioms are used when one refers to one book, one person, one year or one pair of chopsticks.

When examining demographic data one should be aware that in some societies people do not know their date of birth nor how old they are. It should also be noted that in some countries age distribution data could be distorted because girls are categorised according to whether or not they have reached puberty.

Also read

- Language
- Religious belief
- Taboos, superstitions and non-religious beliefs

PERCEPTION OF SPACE

People's perception of space is typically influenced and conditioned by factors which include the size of a country, its physical structure as well as its population density. This is not quite as simple as it sounds since for practical reasons the general public may be forced to surrender its physical privacy when using public transport such as buses, ferries, trams and trains, but never-the-less still implement it in their home and at work. Perception of space is reflected by the degree of physical contact and proximity between people which may be different between friends than with outsiders. It may be reflected to a different extent in the use of body language when queuing.

In some cultures, space reveals status and power. An exclusive, individual or private office has higher status than one that is shared or working in an open-plan office. In countries such as the United States, Germany and the Netherlands, the location of an office within a building and size of an office can be used as an indicator as to the status of an executive, although in the United Kingdom and in Scandinavia there is nowadays greater acceptance of open-plan offices.

In Japan many offices are commonly arranged with the desk of the person in charge at the end of a row of desks which have been pushed together for use by junior employees, in order to maximise his interaction with them, while in North American corporate offices the person in charge is usually physically isolated in a separate private room.

In some offices in France it is more likely that the centre or central desk along the wall is occupied by the person who is in the key position, as in France control is usually associated with the centre. It is important to be aware that there are many countries where such status symbols do not apply, and it is quite possible to come to an incorrect conclusions as to a person's status within an organisation, if one applied the same criteria as operating in one's own country. One should also bear in mind that it may be health and safety regulations or practical factors or criteria regarding daylight or sunlight that may have influenced the location and design of offices, and not culture related factors.

Indirectly related to space is the question of privacy. There are culture related differences between those companies that operate an *open door* policy and those that adopt a *closed door* management style. These culture related variances do not necessarily imply that the persons automatically adhere to a particular style of management, or that they want to keep secrets from one another, but it is more likely to show that persons working in a closed door context prefer to operate without group consultation. Associated with these images are other culture related courtesies such as whether or not to knock on an office door even by colleagues working within the same company and then waiting to be invited to enter, rather than just walking into the person's room.

The size of homes and dwellings has considerable bearing on buying patterns and habits not just for home furnishing but also for food. For example, consumers in the USA usually have larger living accommodation than consumers in Japan. In the United States consumers tend to go shopping for food much less frequently than those living in Japan where accommodation and particularly space for storage of food is much and it would therefore be bought more frequently and in smaller quantity. Size and space can therefore have a wide range of marketing implications for the food manufacturing and distribution industry.

Also read

- Body language and non-verbal communication
- Business ideology, management style and decision making
- Food, drink and eating lifestyle
- Taboos, superstitions and non-religious beliefs

PHOTOGRAPHY, VIDEO AND OTHER FORMS OF VISUAL RECORDINGS

When visiting other countries visitors usually take photographs or visual recordings of colourful and picturesque scenes of people and their surroundings.

In many countries it is prohibited to photograph any site or area even remotely connected with defence and related installations. In some countries there are other sites and structures that might well be considered by the national authorities as being defence related. These might include road and railway bridges, railway stations, docks, airports, public buildings, power stations, factories and even official residences and palaces. As to what is and what is not included under the heading of *sensitive* structures, may well be subject to very wide interpretation. This prohibition may even include military personnel, police, customs and immigration officials. There are also countries, particularly in the Middle East, where it is unwise photograph religious buildings and structures, unless permission has been sought and obtained.

In 2001 a group of aircraft spotters, persons considered in most Western Culture countries to be harmless enthusiasts and usually welcomed with open arms at military and civil air displays, were arrested and charged with espionage for taking photographs at an airshow at a military aerodrome in Greece. The legal proceedings dragged on for several months.

In some countries authorities may not like photographs being taken which focus on the backwardness of their country for example dilapidated local housing conditions or signs of social decay such as intoxicated persons sprawling over pavements or in other public places.

Within counties there may well be groups of people who are very sensitive about having their photographs taken. This sensitivity may be based on their religious or non-religious beliefs. One should not attempt to take their pictures without seeking their permission which may well be refused. Likewise in some countries it is advisable that male visitors do not try to take photograph of local womenfolk, although the same women might on occasions not object if their photograph was taken by woman visitor.

There is a tale of some tourists to an African country who had just stepped off their bus, and were watching a number of young local women weaving carpets in a roadside shed. One of the tourist pointed his camera at the weaving women and one, who had become aware of this shouted at him and made signs with her hand, which he interpreted as waving him off. As the discomfited tourist was about to apologise to the tour guide for trying to take a photograph without asking their permission, the guide said, 'she is trying to tell you that you have left the cap on your lens.'

Also read

- Censorship
- Verbal and visual presentations

POLITICS

Unless one is a politician or on a political mission it is unwise, when visiting some countries, to get involved in or to discuss politics. The same applies to discussing religion-related subjects when visiting countries where freedom of religion does not exist or where there is intolerance of other religions. Singing praises of the virtues of one's own society and highlighting the faults of the host country is not only discourteous but will cause resentment and may lead to offence being taken.

There are some countries where records of past and notable events may have been modified and altered in line with changes in the political environment of a country. This might not only refer to national events such as revolutions and uprisings, but relate to actions by individuals, groups of people or even large segments of the population, like ethnic minorities.

Likewise, in some countries, after a change in government, the officially approved version of a nation's history may be changed. This could manifest itself in many different ways. The names of streets and even of towns may be changed, maps may be re-drawn or withdrawn, books by certain authors may be banned or even burned, particular newspapers and magazines may be censored, or prohibited from being imported or distributed. While only some of these situations may be relevant to a visitor, ignorance of these facts could lead to a faux pas or have even more unfortunate consequences, like imprisonment.

In one particular Mediterranean country, the manager of a foreign airline office was imprisoned for several months for possessing and displaying in his office a globe of the world on which a particular province of that country was shown as an independent political entity. The fact that this globe was almost an antique was not considered relevant. The official view of the country was that this particular province had never existed as an independent political entity.

In another country difficulties arose when the local language edition of the Encyclopaedia Britannica was on display for sale and it was found that one of the statements 'that various towns in that country were under the rule of a particular ethnic minority during the Middle Ages', could be interpreted as 'weakening national view' of the country. This resulted in that particular edition of the Encyclopaedia having to be withdrawn.

Some countries apply, for reasons perhaps related to security and defence but probably just basic mistrust, a range of modes of secrecy and concealment. These may take the form of maps being altered so that whole districts are transposed and even the position and location of buildings, roads, railways and rivers being altered. Possession of a non-approved map may lead to difficulties with law enforcement agencies in these countries.

Also read

- Censorship
- Religious beliefs

PROTOCOL AND CONVENTIONS RELATED TO OFFICIAL OCCASIONS

Usually this is understood to refer to the activities and arrangements on a governmental level for planning and executing events of national significance. It would, for example, provide guidelines for managing visits by foreign dignitaries as well as for organising national celebrations. However protocol is also very relevant to non-governmental organisations particularly to companies and organisations trading with or operating in other countries. Executives should be aware of etiquette and conventions connected with receiving foreign visitors to ensure that their visits are managed with minimum friction and maximum efficiency. It is also to ensure that executives and others, including tourists, visiting foreign countries understand the customs and way of life of people in the countries which they intend to visit.

When planning international conferences one should be aware that there are many issues relating to protocol. These include, for example, seating arrangements for participants. Are they to be seated according to diplomatic precedence, by personal rank or status or by nationality? If by nationality will seating arrangements be by country, in alphabetical order? If this is to be the procedure will the alphabetical order of country names be based on English or another language?

While it is established practice for government departments to have officials responsible for protocol, only a few of the larger international and national companies and corporations retain qualified specialists or protocol officers.

Any organisation whose executives often travel to foreign countries, receive foreign visitors, or export, advertise and promote their products and services in foreign countries should consider creating of a focal point within their organisation such as a library or data bank, where information about how to interact with persons from other countries is collected. It is important that the information is kept up-to-date and be available to everyone in the organisation. Alternatively, an organisation might appoint a member of the staff who will act as a focal point within the organisation, to give advice on such matters.

Duties of such a person or protocol officer might include giving advice on receiving and entertaining foreign visitors, business protocol, appropriate attire for business meetings, negotiating style, selection of gifts, and many of the other subjects covered by this book. Their duties would also include providing advice to personnel prior to travelling to other countries.

At a press conference shortly after he was named secretary of state in 1973, Henry Kissinger was asked whether he preferred being addressed as 'Mr. Secretary' or 'Dr. Secretary'. 'I don't stand on protocol,' Kissinger playfully replied. 'If you will just call me 'Excellency,' it will be okay.'

Also read

- Culture

Punctuality, Duration and Terminating a Business Visit

Whether or not one should be punctual for an appointment is very much culture related. In most Western European countries, some of the Eastern European countries and in North America punctuality for both business and social appointments is most important. Appointments are planned for practically every working minute of the day, sometimes even weeks ahead and a fully booked diary is almost a status symbol.

The story goes that a Greek asks his Swiss partner, 'Why are you so angry because I arrived at 9.30?'
'Because', replies the Swiss 'it says 9 o'clock in my diary'.
'Then why don't you write 9.30 in your diary and then we will both be happy' was the rational response by the Greek.

There are however many countries where people have a different perception or sense of time and priorities. Personal issues may, for example, take priority over business appointments. In some countries it may be acceptable and perhaps even expected to arrive between five and ten minutes late. In other societies where arrival 'within the hour' is customary there would be no reason to apologise if one arrived for a meeting within this period.

The length of time allocated to an meeting depends on the relative importance the parties concerned attach to a meeting, and an hour spent with an important person has greater significance than if only half an hour was scheduled for the same meeting. Conventions for ending a business visit or meeting very much depend on the customs and practices of country and the status of the person one is visiting. Sometimes it is the senior of the two parties who indicates that the visit is over. In practice the majority of visits are often ended by mutual agreement. In Western culture countries, when making an appointment, it is often prudent to ascertain how much time can be or has been allocated to the meeting. Some indication of time-frame can often be established by having an off-the-record conversation with the person's secretary or personal assistant. An indication of this will also help the visitor to establish how much time might be available for preliminaries or pleasantries and how much on the purpose for the visit.

Also read

- Appointments
- Business meetings
- Measuring and managing time
- Sense of time
- The family and the in-group

Religious Beliefs

Religion is often defined as a socially shared set of beliefs, ideas and actions which relate to a reality that cannot be verified empirically, yet is believed to affect the course of natural and human events. Because such beliefs condition people's motivations and priorities, it affects their thoughts and actions including their behaviour.

From a business person's point of view, it is important to note that religious beliefs affect not only the political and economic environment of a country, but also many aspects of commercial and business operations, consumption patterns and the personal conduct and behaviour of individuals. At the heart of the Islamic religion, for example, is the concept that the first law for man to obey is the law of God, not the law of the State. This means that what in one country might be expected to be purely an economic matter and discussed and negotiated within such a framework, becomes in another country a religious one and visitors from Western culture countries soon discover that their usual reference points are no longer applicable.

There are numerous religions and religious groups in the world. The main adherents of literate religions are Buddhist, Christian (including Roman Catholic, Protestant, Anglican and Eastern Orthodox), Hindu, Muslim and others which include Sikh, Jewish, Confucian, Shinto, Baha'i, Parseeism and Zoroastrian. Non-literate religions include Chinese Folk religion, Tribalists, and Shamanists. In addition to these there are also many millions of non-religious persons and atheists.

One should be aware that there is unlikely to be complete religious homogeneity in a country, as there are people, sects and groups within most religions who place different interpretations on the requirements of their religion, and whose religious practices may therefore not conform to standard practices of their particular religion. Therefore stereotype conclusions about the impact of religion both nationally and worldwide should be guarded against.

Aspects of day-to-day life which may be affected by religious beliefs include food which may or may not be eaten; how food is to be prepared and as well as periods of fasting and feasting; whether alcohol may or may not be consumed; whether or not tobacco may be smoked; the trades and professions one can follow; work schedules which must make allowances for prayer periods; religious festivals; leisure activities and whether gambling is permitted; the type of garments and apparel which must be worn in religious or holy places, in public places and in the home; and the social and economic role of women.

To import products such as pigskin gloves and liqueur-filled chocolates into countries where in accordance with religious beliefs, to eat pork and to drink alcohol is strictly forbidden, might be obvious. One should also bear in mind that to present someone in India where cows are sacred, with a picture enclosed in a beautiful cowhide picture frame likely to give offence, as would be the gift of a bottle of whisky to someone in Saudi Arabia.

Religion has implications in many other fields. Here are some examples — the attitude to life of some religions does not encourage materialism and consumerism; finance, where religious beliefs determine banking transactions that is, whether interest can be earned and paid; whether and how a commercial debt can be collected; personal taxation; it may affect work ethics and performance and respect for those who are their seniors, and prohibits the challenging of authority; similarly whether the rewards for merit or work is to be now or in the afterlife; in the legal sector where the commercial law may be an extension of religious law rather than of civil or common law; in employee relations where it could have a bearing on the employment of co-religionists, employment of members of the extended family and other forms of nepotism, also ethics regarding duties and responsibilities for one's employees; advertising — what can and cannot be advertised and its method of presentation.

Under Sharia law, which governs the lives of the followers of Islam, investors are not allowed to hold stakes in bank or insurance companies because they are usurious. Nor are they allowed to buy shares in companies whose main business is alcohol, pork processing, defence, gambling or entertainment. Where religious beliefs determine banking operations, that is whether interest can be earned and paid, there are still some disagreements among banking institutions, as to what is and is not Sharia-compliant. There is for example a divide between the Middle Eastern states where there is strict interpretation of Sharia law compared with its understanding in South East Asia.

Religion has also effected the conduct of war. During the period of Ramadan (the daily fast between sunrise and sunset practised during Ramadan) in some of the 20th century wars in the Arab world there were unwritten rules which both side followed under their respective Arab leadership. To non-Arabs these rules might well be compared to the concepts of chivalry as used to be observed in Western culture countries.

Religious divisions within countries can create both social and commercial opportunities and problems, particularly where there is antipathy between religious groups. The consequences of such divisions sometimes result, in addition to different places of worship, in separate and parallel organisations and communities.

Other consequences include separate schools, clubs, political parties, trade unions, financial institutions, newspapers, radio and TV stations, and even shopping centres. In a suburb of Tel Aviv in Israel which has a high concentration of ultra-orthodox Jews a shopping centre has been opened without coffee bars or a cinema, to guard against unnecessary fraternisation between men and women. Its second floor bans men. All mannequins are headless, because of the religious edit against any likeness of the human image. The bedding department has only single beds because even married ultra-orthodox couple must sleep separately.

Nearly every religion has symbols which are held sacred by its followers and these images must be treated with respect. Mistreating or insulting an image can not only give great offence, but can result in prosecution of offenders. It is therefore important to ascertain whether or not a sacred image or symbol can be used as souvenirs or as a work of art, or even more importantly, whether it would cause offence if it were used as a form of embellishment as part of an object of merchandise. There may also be restrictions on specific letters, monograms, words, names and terms associated with religious or non-religious beliefs, and whether they can be used in conjunction with merchandise and services.

Also read

- Alcohol
- Smoking
- Taboos, superstitions and non-religious beliefs
- The way of life, lifestyle or quality of life

Sense of Humour, Laughter and Smiles

Humour, if wisely used, can be a powerful sales aid to persons engaged in business. It can, however, seldom be exported successfully. An example is a humorous Western European advertising and promotion film which shows chocolates jumping out of a box. It will probably not be understood by many seeing this film in some African or Asian or Middle Eastern countries who may think 'chocolates don't normally jump out of boxes, either this is magic or just plain silly, better not buy these chocolates'.

In almost every country there is at least one national minority group who serve as the laughing-stock or target for jokes, but it is, hardly likely that a British person would understand jokes made in Germany about Swabians, nor would a German understand a British joke about the Irish. Unless one is absolutely certain that the person with whom one is conversing has a similar social and cultural background, it is usually not advisable for a visitor to attempt to tell a joke or an amusing story in another country or to an audience from a different cultural background. One should bear this in mind when making a speech in a foreign country.

Many years ago a postcard was on sale in Belgian and its caption read 'The Perfect European should be...' There were small caricatures of the citizens of the (then) 12 European member states, each with a brief title:

sober — as the Irish
generous — as a Dutchman
cooking — like a Brit
controlled — as an Italian
available — as a Belgian
humorous — as a German
driving — like the French
humble — as a Spaniard
famous — as a Luxembourger
technical — as a Portuguese
discreet — as a Dane and lastly
organised — as a Greek

Laughter and smiles can have different cultural meanings. It can mean anything from happiness and joy in Western culture societies, to a conventional formula for hiding embarrassment, nervousness and shyness in some Asian countries, as in Japan for example.

Also read

- Jokes and anecdotes
- Using proverbs

SENSE OF TIME

Every culture has its own perception of the significance of time, and while some cultures consider punctuality a virtue others treat it more casually.

In some countries there is a tradition that the time required for a decision is directly proportional to its importance. To make, what would appear to a foreign visitor, an apparently minor decision may take a local person an inordinately long time. If a foreigner, in all sincerity, tries and speed up the process it could well result in a perceived reduction in the status of the person concerned, irrespective whether he is a government official or a business executive. In some cultures, to set someone a deadline during negotiations may well be considered impolite, pushing or derogatory and it is likely to be counter-productive.

There are countries, where the time required to get something accomplished depends on the degree of relationship with the person concerned. The closer the relationship the faster the service, and really close relatives may well take absolute priority. This can be a reason why, having made a firm appointment in, say, an Asian or Middle Eastern country, a visitor has been kept waiting, because the person who has granted the interview may consider it far more rude to tell the visitor, probably a relative, with whom is currently conversing that his time is up, than to keep the foreign visitor waiting.

Time, in many countries in the Arab world for example, is not their personal possession. It is a commodity controlled by outside forces — God and the family-based society and therefore something about which the individual cannot and should not be unduly concerned.

Sense of time is the theme of many amusing stories. When a Spanish ambassador said to his Irish opposite number: 'Tell me, do the Irish understand the Spanish concept of 'manana'?' The Irish ambassador replied doubtfully, 'Yes, but nothing so precise'.

There are different attitudes to future time. While in Western culture countries planning for the future is normal, in some cultures the future, even if in the format of a five or ten year business plan, is too far away to be of significance and therefore difficult even to consider or reflect upon. This often results in local officials and businesspersons not wishing to engage in forward planning, sometimes quoting what may appear to Western culture executives, unrealistic lead-times.

Also read

- Appointments
- Measuring and managing time
- Punctuality, duration and terminating a business visit

SEX

Attitudes towards sexual morality are very much conditioned by the culture, social morals and religions of countries. There are also different attitudes of morality for men and women. In Christian Western countries, and particularly in those imbued with Puritan Christian concepts, sex is looked upon as basically sinful and monogamy and abstinence as moral virtues. In many other societies, for example Japan, sex never had the stigma of evil or the sense of guilt.

What should be noted is that there are some countries where it is unwise to engage in extra-marital sexual or homosexual activities, since it is not unknown for foreign visitors, as a result of such encounters, to be blackmailed and then held to ransom for their company's or government's commercial or political secrets or for other reasons.

In a number of countries, particularly in the Middle East people are expected to respect local culture, traditions and laws. Acts of public affection between men, between women and between men and women, which includes embracing and kissing, constitute a public order offence which would lead to arrest and punishment. Other public order offences may include cross-dressing and topless sunbathing.

In most countries sexual relations with a person under the age of consent is normally a criminal offence with varying degrees of punishment. The age of consent varies from country to country and in the United States even from State to State. A worldwide list of countries with the minimum age of consent for heterosexual, homosexual and lesbian relations has been published by an international AIDS charity.

In some Muslim countries extra-marital sexual and homosexual activities are punishable by death.

One should also be aware of the operation of organisations such as The Women's Rights activists in many countries. Some of these organisations would like to have sexual harassment defined along lines proposed by the European Community Code which is: Unwanted conduct of a sexual nature or other conduct based on sex affecting the dignity of women and men at work, including unwelcome physical, verbal or non-verbal conduct.

Also read

- Laws and legal systems
- Male-female relationships
- Social kissing
- Women in business and the professions

Signs, Pictorial Representations, Emoticons and Other Symbols

Signs, pictorial representations, emoticons and other symbols serve a wide range of purposes and appear in countless shapes and forms. Hundreds of thousands are in use, worldwide. Commercially they are used as trademarks and may be associated with patents. They are used as corporate and company logos. They feature as national symbols and in flags and banners. As heraldic devices they are used by noble families and by commercial undertakings. They feature as icons in religious environments. Their shapes may comprise graphic designs incorporating alphabetic forms and concrete forms, for example as people, plants, animals as well as astrological or heavenly bodies. In their abstract form they include circles, spirals and squares. They also make use of numbers and letters.

There is a basic difference between signs and symbols. Signs signify or stand for something, whilst symbols represent something else by association or resemblance, for example peace is often represented by an olive branch, or a dove or a rainbow. One should be aware that signs and symbols even if traditionally endowed with a special meaning in one culture or country are sometimes imbued with different meaning or significance in other cultures and countries. It would be unwise to use signs, pictorial representations, emoticons and other symbols if they are likely to offend national or local sensitivities. On the other hand one should consider their use if they had a favourable connotation or meaning. It is therefore essential to undertake research before using them in connection with products and services in other countries or cultures.

When preparing public relation or advertising material for some of the non-secular countries in the world, for instance some of the countries located in Arabian Gulf and the Middle East, it is essential to avoid the use of the Christian symbols such as an angel or a cross or perhaps even a plus sign, and similarly a six-pointed star that could be mistaken for the Star of David.

Some symbols have negative and adverse values, while others have strong positive ones. In Japan the tortoise symbolises long life and good fortune. The crane is regarded in Japan as lucky since folklore states that it lives for a thousand years, and to use this bird in trademarks for food and beverage products is claimed to be advantageous. In a Scandinavian country the entrance to a brewery is flanked by two statues of elephants and these are shown on the labels of its Elephant Beer. When seeking to export to an African market, research established that a pair of elephants was a local symbol of bad luck and it was considered unlikely that anyone would drink from a bottle that might have an association with bad luck. The problem was resolved by adding a third elephant to the label.

Compared with face-to-face communication and telephone communication non-verbal signal or prompts are absent when using the electronic media, such as email, text and multimedia messages, or MMS. Non-verbal cues include tone of voice and body language. Whilst telephone users can make use of tone of voice to indicate anger or humour to supplement their message, users of the electronic media have long realised that such means were not available to them and that their absence sometimes led to unfavourable results, such as misunderstandings, indignation or even offence being taken. This was partially resolved through the creation of special symbols known as emoticons and smileys. Emoticons are symbols or combinations of symbols used to convey the emotional contents of a communication in a written format.

A typical example is :-) which is described as a 'classic smile with nose'. Many others are now used. Western emoticons are composed to be read horizontally, that is from left to right; the eyes (the colon punctuation mark) are on the left, followed by symbols for the nose and the mouth. Japanese emoticons however are formed to be read vertically. One should be aware that the use of Japanese anime emoticons has become more widespread. There are many emoticon variants, the factors controlling the range of graphics, symbols, characters and fonts accessible are computer hardware and software and lastly, human inventiveness. Many additional graphics, symbols, characters and fonts are available in other languages. The ever growing market for computer games has resulted in an increased use of moving graphical emoticons.

There is already a wide range of signs and symbols which are part of a new, international pictorial marking language. They include road signs, the symbol of the International Olympic Movement, international airports, currency exchange points, railway stations, toilets as well as safety signs and hazard symbols.

Many signs and symbols are used by exporters of goods and applied to packaging containers. Although widely known and generally understood they have not yet been internationally standardised. They include an image of rain drops falling on an umbrella indicating that the package should be kept dry and protected from rain, and the symbol of a broken wine glass signifying that the goods inside the package are fragile.

There are never-the-less occasions when even simple symbols and signs are not understood nor interpreted as intended. This occurred when dockworkers at a small port in Africa were about to unload boxes marked with the broken wine glass symbols, one of the established signs for 'fragile goods'. The dockworkers however assumed that these boxes contained broken glass and dumped all boxes into the sea.

Many pictographs, signs and symbols which are used in some countries are not accepted in others, where their use could lead to misunderstandings and sometimes even culturally embarrassing situations. For example, the symbols used in most Western culture countries for women's toilets are unacceptable in some countries in the Arabian Gulf region, because the symbolic silhouette of the female figure on doors of women's toilets shows too much of the legs and should, in accordance with their customs, be shown wearing traditional ankle-length clothes.

Also read

- Email, netiquette and cyberspace behaviour
- Flowers and giving flowers
- Information, operating instructions and methods of use
- Trade fairs and exhibitions

SMOKING

In a large number of countries it is forbidden to smoke not only in public buildings but also in offices, shops and factories. There may be local regulation regarding smoking in hotels, restaurants, bars and places of entertainment, and the smoking ban may also include public transport and taxis.

There may also exist local customs and regulations concerning the smoking of particular tobacco products — cigarettes, herbal cigarettes, cheroots, cigars and pipes, and conventions applicable to taking snuff, using chewing tobacco and taking and using other substances. In many South East Asian and the Pacific region countries people chew betel nut (actually areca nut and betel leaf). Customs and rituals associated with this include its disposal by spitting, which may be disconcerting to fastidious foreigners. The equivalent Western culture custom is chewing gum which is similarly associated with displeasing disposal problems.

Hookah smoking is practiced in many countries, particularly in the Middle East. These may be single or multi-stemmed water pipe devices for smoking tobacco or non-tobacco ingredients. Before smoking a hookah one should acquaint oneself with local hookah smoking customs and conventions.

There are people who object to being in a car with someone who is smoking and permission should therefore be sought before lighting up. In some cars, small notices or signs are sometimes displayed, indicating that smoking is not permitted.

In most societies there are well established customs and conventions which determine whether it is and when it is permitted to smoke before, during or after a meal. Customs may differ according to whether the meal is in a private house, in a restaurant or part of a formal or ceremonial occasion, and one should always make discrete enquiries before lighting up.

The tale is told that the American slogan for Salem cigarettes, 'Salem — Feeling Free,' was translated in Japan into 'When smoking Salem, you feel so refreshed that your mind seems to be free and empty.'

Also read

- Business entertaining
- Leisure and leisure activities

Social Contact

In some societies social events such as receptions, cocktail parties, luncheons, are primarily for sociable and friendly activities and not an extension of business activities and they should not be used for business-related conversations unless this is initiated by one's host. There are however other functions, described as corporate hospitality events. The prime object of most of these is to encourage business-related conversations in a pleasant and relaxed atmosphere.

There are many subtleties regarding invitations to visit the home of a business person in another country and it is important to be aware of the difference between what is a casual friendly remark and what is really a serious and genuine invitation.

In some of those countries where casual or informal entertaining between persons in a business or governmental relationship does not exist, official receptions and banquets may well be the only form of social contact.

There are still many occasions, in Middle Eastern and Arabian countries for example, where official receptions are for men only and if women are invited, the sexes tend to separate.

Just as in some societies the term 'brother' may have different meanings, likewise the word 'friend'. In some countries, for example the United States, those with whom one has business dealings or socialises or works with would be called friends rather than business acquaintances, which would be the case in many other cultures. Under these circumstances friendships are more easily made and likewise dissolved than in other societies, and this can give rise to misinterpretation and hurt feelings by those not familiar with these particular forms of conventions. This type of friendship, combined with a greater degree of natural informality also manifests itself in the way persons address each other. It includes addressing foreign visitors whom they have only recently met, by their first or given name, a practice which often bewilders and sometimes perturbs and disconcerts those from more formal societies. This degree of informality is not confined to the United States and is increasingly found among younger members of the business community in many Western culture countries.

Also read

- Business entertaining
- Links and connections

SOCIAL KISSING

In some countries kissing is a substitute for the handshake or the formal slight bow as the usual form of greeting. In Western culture countries social kissing is usually, but not exclusively, reserved for social meetings and greetings, it is also frequently practised among those connected with the entertainment and the fashion industries, and the media.

One of the major problems that arise from social kissing is its perception by the parties concerned. In France, 'la bise' means no more than the equivalent of 'hello', to persons from countries not used to this form of greeting it may however suggest a special or close relationship which could result in misinterpretation.

Social kissing takes many forms. In the United Kingdom for example, babies are kissed on the head, while injuries to young children are immediately made better by kissing the injured spot. During the run-up to elections when canvassing for votes politicians make a beeline for women holding babies and kissing as many of these (babies only) as possible. Brides are traditionally kissed by the best man and dice are kissed for luck. Christmas time provides a unique opportunity for social kissing and even strangers are permitted to kiss members of the family and other guests under the mistletoe.

Kissing ladies on one or both cheeks has been a British custom for at least 500 years. The Dutch academic Erasmus (1466 or 1469–1536) when he first visited England wrote: *'The English have one practice which cannot be too much admired. When you go anywhere on a visit the girls kiss you. They kiss you when you arrive; they kiss you when you leave; and they kiss you again when you return. Go where you will, it is all kisses.'*

Quite a normal practice is cheek-to-cheek kissing, which may or may not be accompanied by smacking noises (sounding like 'Mwa! Mwa!') as kisses are exchanged. A variant of this is air kissing where two persons put their cheeks in close proximity but without touching each other and making kissing-like sounds.

The number of kisses exchanged range from a single kiss, to two, three and even up to four. In many countries one might start with the left cheek, followed by right cheek and then left and then right again according to degree of relationship, or intimacy, and of course the custom of the country or the society.

Hand kissing is popular in some countries, for example in Austria, but practiced more often by older men. In this case the man

does not let his lips touch the lady's hand, but hovers a thumb's width (or just a few centimetres) above it. Local customs in some countries may decree whether single as well as married ladies may be greeted in this manner.

Social kissing is not necessarily restricted to male greeting female or female greeting female. In some countries men traditionally greet each other by kissing each other on the cheek or mouth, or on the bridge of the nose, or the forehead without any insinuation of homosexuality.

In practically every country there are clearly understood protocols and customs which determine business, social and political kissing. In Russia for example, among friends man to man kissing when greeting one another is the norm. In Iran men of unequal status kiss on the cheek while those of equal status kiss on the mouth. If however there is any element of doubt, it would be better to adhere to more conventional forms of greeting, be it a handshake or a bow. The story goes that an Italian commented to a friend that in England the practice of male kissing was thought to be a sign of dangerous effeminacy. He said 'The reason why Englishmen don't like kissing each other is, that so many of you are really homosexual, and you are afraid you might get carried away.'

Social kissing is not restricted purely to greetings but also when leave-taking.

In addition to social kissing there is also the practice of kissing as a sign of respect and often this is associated with religious practices. This includes followers of the Catholic faith who pay respect to the Pope by kneeling before him and kissing his ring and the ancient custom of kissing ring of a Bishop. Those who are Eastern Orthodox Christians kiss an icon when entering a church. Religious Jews who kiss the Western wall of the Holy Temple in Jerusalem Hindus who sometimes kiss the ground of a temple and Muslims who kiss the Black Stone during their Hajj pilgrimage to Mecca.

Also read

- Greeting, introductions, modes of address and leave-taking
- Male-female relationships
- Names

STATUS SYMBOLS

The early impression or the image a visitor is able to create during his initial meeting with the person he is visiting in another country often determines the course of their future relationship and naturally the converse also applies.

Most persons tend to judge their foreign contacts on the basis of their own status symbols. Such symbols might include any of the following: a name or title indicating tradition, privilege or wealth; education for example schools, universities or other educational establishments attended; dress and appearance — quality and style of clothing and accessories and in the case of men whether clean-shaven or with designer stubble or bearded. Personal contacts; material symbols such as location, size and decor of an office; brand and type of car; brand or logo of briefcase; the brand of fountain pen or wrist watch; the name of one's tailor or dress designer, jeweller and shoemaker; the quality of one's business card and company stationery — whether or not embossed.

In every culture and country something is likely to be a status symbol or an image enhancer. Whether, however, it creates the desired, positive, negative or any kind of effect is culture related and depends very much whether, for example, the other person sets much store by professional qualifications, academic achievements, being well connected, the ownership of a collection of paintings, a Rolls-Royce, a Cadillac, or even a football club.

It should not be overlooked that there are societies where emphasis on material possessions is frowned upon and in that event any reference to wealth might result in creating an negative or adverse image.

As a generalisation, and taking only three countries as an example, senior officials and executives in France are more likely to be impressed with a person's academic or educational background and achievements. In Germany and Austria, these would include both professional and academic qualifications which should be shown on one's business card.

In the United Kingdom it might be achievement in the field of sport or memberships of an exclusive club, it might also include education but probably only if it was an exclusive public school, a prestigious university or college or business school.

In the Middle East many businessmen were unlikely to use location, size and furnishing of their office as part of their status symbol system, but this is slowly changing as more Western business culture status symbols are adopted. These businessmen may however discreetly refer to other symbols such as family connections or friendship links to the great and good.

When meeting a foreign executive for the first time there are likely to be advantages if both parties share some common interests. Often this is only discovered during introductory conversation more by luck than by design, but proves the value of taking at least a little time to get to know the other person. Luck, however, is an unpredictable commodity and it is a good investment of time to research the background or CV (curriculum vitae) of the person one is scheduled to meet, to identify potential areas of common interests. One must however be aware that while it would be considered quite normal to talk about one's personal life in some countries and cultures, for example in many Western culture societies, this is to be avoided in other countries such as Korea.

Being familiar with the cultural heritage of the country one is visiting or at least having some background information about it, is likely to create a favourable impression. Such information could for example include a country's standing in the world of sport.

It almost always creates a good impression to speak just a few words of the language of the country one is visiting, even if these are limited to expressions of greetings and gratitude.

If staying in hotels, particularly if they are also to be used for business meetings, the locally perceived ranking, grade or class of the hotel may influence the positive but also the negative perception of the local business community regarding the status of the foreign visitor and his organisation. It is important to decide what image one wishes to convey and to understand how this image might be perceived by the local business community. Staying in a very low category hotel may convey an image of an unimportant organisation, whilst a 5-star hotel might suggest that its products and services could be overpriced.

Also read

- Achievements
- Business cards
- Class systems, caste and social structure
- Conversation and communication
- Dress code and etiquette
- Perception of space

TABLE ETIQUETTE AND EATING

While in some countries it is customary to arrive on time for a meal, in others it is much more appropriate to arrive at well after the stated time.

The time at which meals are taken vary considerably between countries, midday meals could start as early as 11.00 hours or as late as 15.00 hours, while evening meals could start at 18.00 hours or on the other hand as late as 22.00 hours. In Norway for example, lunch which consists of a very light meal, is usually a half-hour break between 11.00 hours and 12.00 hours, while 'middag', the main meal of the day is usually taken around 17.00 hours.

Almost everywhere there are conventions or protocols regarding the seating of guests and hosts, toasts and speeches on formal meal occasions. It is customary in some of the Scandinavian countries, for example, for the host to propose a toast of welcome at the beginning of a meal and only after this should the guest drink and propose another toast.

In some countries and in some societies there may be religious customs associated with meal occasions such as the 'breaking of bread and eating it' at the start of a meal or a short prayer before and/or after a meal.

One should be mindful of the religious beliefs of both hosts and guests in order not to cause offence by offering food and drink which they may be forbidden to touch and consume.

Knives and forks are used for eating in most but not all countries. There are countries in the Far East, including China and Japan, where chopsticks are used. In yet others in Asia, Africa and the Middle East where it is customary to eat with one's fingers, but use only the right hand and not the left hand. Proficiency with chopsticks in those countries where chopsticks are used, and being able to eat with one's fingers in those countries where one eats in this way is a distinct advantage, it gives a good impression and could be a contributing factor to a successful relationship.

In some restaurants in France it is customary to retain the same set of cutlery for each course, while in others the used cutlery is removed after each course. Cultural differences apply when one wishes to indicate that one has finished a course or a meal. Placing the knife and fork, laid together, diagonally across the middle of the plate signifies that one has finished in some countries and that the plate can be taken away. In others this would not be understood, since their way of indicating that one has finished eating is to leave the knife and fork crossed on the plate.

There is the tale of a foreign business executive being invited by his host to a very exclusive London restaurant. Since asparagus and certain other foods are traditionally eaten with one's fingertips, small silver fingerbowls with containing water and a small slice of lemon were placed in front of each of them, so that they could rinse their fingers at the end of the course. After a little while the visitor raised his fingerbowl and drank part of the contents. His host, to be polite, raised his own fingerbowl in a toast to him and then also drank.

In every country there are conventions which determine when it is appropriate to leave after a meal. In Kuwait, for example, whether invited to a meal in a private house or to an official dinner in a hotel, it is customary for guests to depart as soon as they have drunk their coffee or tea. In private houses this sometimes leads to meals being served at a very late hour, since out of politeness the hosts do not like their guests to depart too early. In China too both host and guests would depart very soon after the last course of the meal had been served and eaten.

Whether visitors should return an invitation after being entertained by their host, either at their hotel or at a restaurant, depends very much on the country being visited and local advice should be sought.

Also read

- Business entertaining
- Food, drink and eating lifestyle
- Religious beliefs

TABOOS, SUPERSTITIONS AND NON-RELIGIOUS BELIEFS

Non-religious beliefs are part of the culture and tradition of every country and will be encountered in various forms and guises everywhere in the world. They include manifestations such as legends, myths and folklore, omens, premonitions and other kinds of divination, palm-reading, clairvoyance, extra sensory perception and other forms of folk religion and while a person from another country may not give credence to them, one would be extremely foolish to make fun of them, or even worse to ignore them.

There are many countries where the rite specialists including functionaries such as rainmakers, astrologers, priests of many kinds, diviners and witch doctors would be invited to give advice and their help may be sought on particular occasions for example a new business venture of a family occasion such as a wedding, or in connection with prestigious construction projects. Not so long ago government officials in Indonesia solicited the assistance specialists in rituals who subsequently succeeded in bringing about favourable weather conditions for a State visit.

Non-religious beliefs can take many forms, sometimes the avoidance of particular inauspicious words, numbers and dates, for example the elimination of row 13 by some airlines, or floor levels or room numbers in hotels; replacing certain letters and words with signs or symbols such as asterisks (***); not walking under ladders; wearing a talisman to ward off the evil eye; the allocation of lucky telephone number combinations to its favoured citizens, while those judged to be inauspicious might be allocated to foreigners; the choice of an appropriate date for commencing a new business venture and even the location or site of a business enterprise.

In Hong Kong and several other South East Asian countries where the ancient Chinese art of Feng Shui is practiced, a master or expert will often be called in to give advice on whether the location of a building or shop is suitable, he will also advise on the day, hour and even the minute of opening in order to launch the venture to an auspicious start. Feng Shui which can also be interpreted as vibes or vibrations, refers to the relationship between nature and ourselves, so that we might live in harmony within our environment.

Numbers play a significant part in superstitions and the perception as to which numbers are lucky or unlucky vary from country to country. In Italy the really unlucky calendar date is Tuesday 17th, while Friday 17th is also unlucky but not quite to the same degree as a Tuesday In many countries Friday the 13th is considered to be unlucky and not an appropriate day for weddings or boarding a ship. In other countries including Greece, Spain and Mexico the unlucky day in Tuesday the 13th. Even a combination of numbers, for example, launching a new product on March, 16th which would be as 3/16 could be considered astrologically auspicious to someone from China. The numeral 3 signifies *alive* and 16 *plenty to eat* and where 316 would signify *as long as you live our business will be lucky and prosperous.*

It is usually for religious but sometimes also on non-religious grounds that some species of animal and other living things are favoured as a source of meat for some societies, whilst for others they are unclean and therefore forbidden food. Such beliefs last for ever. To the Pacific islanders the meat of pigs and dogs was the mainstay of their lives, whilst to Muslims and Jews it is forbidden food. In Europe the dog has not been eaten during the Christian era except under condition of extreme famine, whilst in some parts of Vietnam they are still available in typical local eating houses. In France horsemeat is part of the national cuisine, whilst people in the United Kingdom would equate this to eating one's best friend.

Many superstitions are associated with sneezing and it was believed that sneezing expels the soul or the breath of life from the body and if one is in the presence of someone who sneezes, one is meant to protect him from danger by uttering appropriate words. The practice of blessing a sneeze dates back many centuries and is known in most cultures and societies. Even in Roman times when someone sneezed people used to say 'long may you live'.

Now-a-days in the United Kingdom when someone sneezes it is customary to say 'bless you'; in German-speaking countries *'Gesundheit'* (health), in Italy *'salute'* (health), and in France *'a tes souhaits'* (to your wishes) to which one should respond with *'merci'* (thank you). Muslims usually say 'All praise be to Allah' or 'May Allah have mercy on you'. Japan is one of the few countries where, when someone sneezes, no comment is made as it is commonly believed that someone is missing the person who sneezed, or talking about them behind their back.

The following rhyme is associated with sneezing in the United Kingdom:

One for sorrow
Two for joy
Three for a letter
Four for a boy
Five for silver
Six for gold
Seven for a secret, never to be told.

And lastly, there is an old English adage which says: *a sneeze before breakfast is a sign that you will hear exciting news before the end of the day.*

Since 1926 the Savoy Hotel in London has kept a three foot high carved black cat called Kaspar. Superstition has it that, at a table of 13 whoever leaves the table earliest is destined to die first. Therefore, at any party of thirteen, Kaspar is placed on the 14th chair to avert catastrophe. A napkin is tied round his neck and he is treated like a bona fide guest. Depending on the generosity of the host, Kaspar is either served a chilled pint of milk or the whole menu, dish after dish, but always with the full complement of china, glass and cutlery.

Also read

- Food, drink and eating lifestyle
- Numbers, figures and counting
- Religious beliefs

TELEPHONING

It should be remembered that the telephone, VoIP (voice of internet protocol) and other internet systems, are often the first contact with a person in a foreign country and the tone of voice one uses becomes not only one's 'face' but also the face of an organization, just as it does with an initial business letter. In some countries it is the practice to have a large number of telephones on the desks of executives, in others all telephone calls are filtered through a personal assistant or a secretary. The tone of voice used on the telephone by executives and officials in some countries may well be very different from what one is used to in one's own country. For example, some people seem to be shouting but this may be because of problems with equipment or transmission or because it is in their nature to do so. It is quite possible that this may appear to be a sign of bad temper to the person on the other end of the line and leads him to think that the other person is rude or discourteous, when in fact it is nothing of the kind.

In some countries the persons answering will give their company's name or their family name, in others only their telephone number or just say 'hello' or the equivalent in their language.

To speak about telephone protocol may sound sophisticated or even fanciful but in most industrialised countries there are conventions and status symbols which should be observed. One should make enquiries about these conventions before asking one's secretary, personal assistant or telephone operator to pass a message to Mr. X or asking them to get Mr. X on the line. For example, if a business meeting is to be arranged in Hong Kong, one would ask one's secretary to make the necessary arrangements. To undertake this task oneself would suggest that one did not have any staff, nor would it give the other party an opportunity to say no without causing offence or losing face.

Telephonic misunderstandings sometimes occur between American and British telephone operators. The American phrase or question 'are you through?' can be interpreted as meaning the same as 'have you finished?', whereas when this question is asked in the United Kingdom by a British operator it usually means 'have you succeeded in making contact so that conversation can start?'

During one of my early visits as a marketing consultant when staying in a hotel in Cairo I tried to telephone a business executive in Alexandria to arrange an appointment. Although I tried a number of times, I could not get through. I then visited the hotel telephone operator and asked for her to help. I had written the number on a piece of paper but after a few minutes she told that the telephone line was out of action. She suggested that I should visit a telephone shop down the road. This I did, but it did not achieve anything either. The shop manager suggested that I should go to the local telephone exchange. This produced a similar result. That evening I mentioned my problem to local person soon put me right. Next day, having written the telephone number on a piece of paper, folded the paper and then placed a US Dollar note inside and gave this to the hotel telephone operator and returned to my room. Shortly afterwards the operator phoned me and said that the line had been repaired and that the person I wish to speak to in Alexandria was at the other end of the line.

There are still some countries where, although they have telephones, there are no telephone directories which can be used to find the number of a private subscriber or organisation and even if there is the telephone directory enquiry office will be unable to provide telephone numbers.

In the telephone directory of Iceland the names of individual Icelanders are listed by their forenames or Christian names in alphabetical order and not by their family or surnames. To assist with identification the directory gives each name in the following sequence — forename, family name, middle name, job title and address. The names of organisations and companies are listed in alphabetical order.

In many countries telephone directory entries are based on company names and family names followed by forename and/or initials, but even in those languages using the romanised script, national telephone directories may not use the same letters as exist in one's own alphabet, and considerable frustration can be caused by one's inability to find names and telephone numbers.

In Finland the letters V and W appear under the same alphabetic heading and the letter Å, followed by Ä and by Ö are the last letters of the alphabet. In the Dutch language there is the additional letter IJ. In the German language the modified vowel or 'umlaut' where two dots are placed over the letters a, o or u (ä, ö and ü). In telephone directories in the United Kingdom M, Mc and Mac are treated as Mac and St is used as an abbreviation for Saint. In some Scandinavian countries where diacritical marks are used on letters such as A and O, one may not find these letters in the same alphabetical order as in the telephone directory in one's own country. When a Thai or a Japanese pronounces a word containing the letter R, the tip of the tongue hits the ridge just behind the upper teeth, and it will not sound like an R to an European ear but more like an L, as a result 'royal' will sound like 'loyal'. The letter H could be pronounced as 'hotel' in English, or silent as in 'otell' in French.

Ways of spelling out a word or name, letter by letter when talking or on the telephone, is not as simple as it might appear as there are many ways of pronouncing individual letters. Even if a phonetic alphabet is used to avoid misunderstanding, there are unfortunately many different phonetic spelling codes in use. The code used worldwide by those associated with civil aviation including pilots and air traffic controllers, is the ICAO (International Civil Aviation Organisation) code. This phonetic code is not however in universal use. In Germany, Austria and Switzerland for example people use other phonetic codes which take into consideration German words including those which incorporate modified vowels or umlauts. The phonetic code for pronouncing the letter 'A' could therefore be: Alpha (ICAO), Anatole (in France), Anton (in Germany), Ancona (in Italy) and Antonio (in Spain). Likewise the letter 'X' could be pronounced as X-RAY or an ICKS (ee-cks). When spelling the letter 'C' for example phonetically as in Canada, one would cause considerable confusion in Germany, since in the German language Canada is spelled with a K, as Kanada.

Because of developments and changes in telecommunication equipment, telephone directories in a number of countries may display special symbols to indicate that specific telephone lines are connected to answering machines and special symbols for fax machines.

Also read

- Forms of address and use of titles
- Greeting, introductions, modes of address and leave-taking
- Language
- Numbers, figures and counting

THE FAMILY AND THE IN-GROUP

Throughout the world there is a wide range of different types of family units such as the single parent family, and the nuclear family consisting of parents and children, both of which are particularly numerous in Western culture countries, as well as units with three generations and extended families. Culture also determines the concept of legitimacy of children and there are many societies which do not subscribe to Western culture view that there is a difference in status between legitimate children and those born out of wedlock or adopted.

Nepotism, or favouritism shown to relatives, especially in appointments to desirable positions, is widespread in many societies, and not only in developing countries. Nepotism is prevalent particularly in those societies where loyalty to family and relatives is strong, where professional management is not widely accepted and where trust in strangers in business is weak. Nepotism is not necessarily negative and in many societies where people are expected to help their relatives it is the local equivalent of social welfare services. It can also be seen as a business model in societies where economic and social relationships are not separated.

In some societies even the words 'brother', 'sister', or 'cousin' have different interpretations. An introduction such as 'this is my brother' may refer to an actual brother, but is just as likely to refer to a cousin or even a friend. An 'uncle' may indicate any senior male relative, and while a cousin might mean a real cousin it could also be used to describe anyone from the same family, tribe or clan. In Asian communities it might include any older adult male respected by the family. Similar conventions are practiced in Western culture countries where in military circles, for example, officers serving in the same regiment might well refer to each other as 'brother officers'. And likewise in conventional family circles where male and female family friends are often introduced to their young children as uncles and aunts.

Within the family ways of demonstrating affection varies from culture to culture, however these differences do not indicate a variation in the quality of affection. It is just that in some cultures families are more physically demonstrative than in others, be this a question of shaking hands, hugging, back-slapping or kissing.

One often hears comments by people from one country about the lack of politeness and rude behaviour of people who may come from or live in another country or community. These comments are often based on observations in a public environment, for instance on public transport such as buses, trams and underground railways, sometimes too when driving a car. What is often not realised is that in many countries there are two sets of social behaviour. One set applies to the in-group, which includes family, friends and other people concerned with that person's welfare, and a very different set of behaviour and attitudes towards the out-group. Within the in-group people are very polite and considerate, while towards the out-group they appear to be ill mannered. Failure to appreciate this difference could result in the mistaken belief that all social behaviour by people in the country concerned is rude and could results in a chain reaction of mutual rudeness, as each party has their worst suspicions about the other party confirmed.

Another form of the 'in-group' is the 'inner-circle', which is often committed to mutual protection and prosperity. Such an in-group could comprise individuals of a similar age, or in China to members of a language dialect group, or in India to members of a caste. In many ways some of the features of these inner circles are perhaps not dissimilar to the 'old boys' network' and networking in Western culture countries.

Also read

- Class systems, caste and social structure
- Links and connections

THE WAY OF LIFE, LIFESTYLE OR THE QUALITY OF LIFE

Cultural factors are responsible for checks and balances relating to lifestyle and quality of life in every country and society. To stray beyond them might place a trendsetter or deviator at risk. Depending on the norms of the society in which a person operates, such risk may include ostracism or even the threat of the death penalty. Particularly if matters concerning religious beliefs or political dogma are challenged.

Societies differ greatly in the extent to which change is perceived favourably. At one extreme a new product, new practice or a new activities may be considered an undesirable disruption of current practices, perhaps even immoral, evil or criminal. At the other extreme, change may be equated with positive or desirable progress.

It is therefore important for executives, officials, consultants or others from another country to be aware of this when they wish to introduce changes into organisations, be this employing expatriates, establishing new procedures, changing routines or bringing in new methodologies.

It is suggested that one should try to identify deterrents to change and decide which cultural obstacles one might be able to modify or adapt. It should be noted that technological changes are usually likely to be accepted much more quickly than social or perceived religious or political changes.

The way of life or a society's attitude towards life style is conditioned and modified by its culture as well as the religious and political beliefs of its population. Should a government, for whatever reason, decide to commit itself to the introduction of a new or a modified form of belief or political system, then the economic and social system of a nation is also likely to be affected. In practical terms this may result not only in changes in the system of taxation and banking transactions, but many other spheres, including the way people transact business, dress and socialise.

Visitors to foreign countries, be they executives or officials are often asked to compare the local quality of life with that of their own country. This is a difficult question to answer since it depends very much on the cultural background of the person who has been asked this question. It raises a number of problems since the perception of quality is related to our personal values and aspirations. An economist will use a different benchmark to that used by a sociologist, or a medical doctor. Some people put a high value on opportunities for happiness including the art of living, such as going to the theatre, to wine or to dine, while others focus on health and longevity, or on income and wealth and whatever money can buy.

Parents in most countries take an emotional pride in their babies and small children, but there are other countries where this may not apply, since parents may be more concerned with a child being yet another mouth to feed. There are a number of countries where a baby boy is greatly preferred to a baby girl, essentially because in time the boy will become a money earner for the family, while money or other economic assets will have to be found by the family for the baby girl to provide a dowry in order to find her a husband at a later stage.

In some societies people are by tradition used to queuing patiently for goods or for services such as public transport. There are also many other countries where this particular feature is completely unknown and pushing, rather than standing in an orderly line, is the normal way of life.

Attitudes to different aspects of personal hygiene are both lifestyle and culture related. In all countries and societies these attitudes determine whether, for example men use grooming products such as soap, toothpaste, deodorants and others. Culture determines the users' perception of these products which may be very dissimilar in different countries. Research undertaken by companies operating in this market sectors established that while toothpaste was perceived as a family health product in the Netherlands and the United Kingdom, it was regarded as a cosmetic product in Greece and Spain.

Also read

- Culture

TIPPING AND GRATUITIES

The practice of giving gratuities or tips is usually determined by custom, telltale signs and unwritten rules. Tipping problems can be reduced to two questions, when and how much. Tips are usually given after a service has been performed however it is not unknown in some countries to have to tip prior to service, for example to secure a good table in a restaurant or to get hold of a taxi. There may be occasions when a tip is given while a service is being performed in a restaurant, such as the preparation and cooking of a special dish next to one's table or carving of a joint of meat by skilled restaurant staff on a trolley positioned next to one's table.

In some restaurants and places of entertainment one may be expected to tip musicians if one has requested that a special tune or melody is played or when they are playing next to one's table.

In some countries tipping is not permitted, while in others it is not expected and in fact positively discouraged because it is contrary to the local concept of hospitality, in yet others nothing can be achieved unless one gives a tip.

Tips may be given for a wide range of services, for instance to a hotel porter for obtaining a taxi or carrying luggage, a waiter for serving a meal, a guide on a tour bus, cabin staff on a cruise liner, a hairdresser or a barber. In principle it is different from gifts and other considerations for some future services, but the dividing line is a very fine one and in some countries almost indistinguishable.

If in doubt about tipping and gratuities, one should make enquiries when making a hotel or restaurant reservation, as to their tipping practice.

Even in those countries where tipping is discouraged, small token gifts typical of one's own country might well be appreciated. It is however essential to be aware of local rules and exercise discretion.

In the United Kingdom, in what are known as Gentlemen's Clubs as well as in Service or Armed Forces Clubs, tipping is not allowed. Instead members are encouraged to contribute to the staff Christmas box. The reason for this is particularly in the Armed Forces or Service Clubs, that all members should receive the same service, regardless of their rank or wealth.

In many countries a service charge or gratuity is include in the hotel and restaurant invoice and additional tipping is not required although sometimes, if there is a small quantity of loose change, this might be left as a tip.

Also read

- Bribery and corruption
- Giving and receiving gifts

TRADE FAIRS AND EXHIBITIONS

All romanised languages are written from left to right and the front of catalogues, brochures and/or price lists when looking at them have the spine or back on their left sides and their opening on their right side. There are however other languages, for instance Arabic and Hebrew, which are written and printed from right to left. In those countries where people read from right to left the front of a catalogue, brochure or price list when looking at it has the spine or back of the publication on its right side and its opening is therefore on the left side. One should be aware of this when designing and printing advertising and promotion material such as catalogues and brochures to be used in countries where the language is written from right to left.

When organising exhibitions in countries where people traditionally read from right to left this must be borne in mind when designing sequential posters and other promotional material to be used on exhibition trade stands. There is the apocryphal story about the pharmaceutical company who used a number of sequential posters to advertise their headache pills at a trade fair in a country in the Arabian Peninsula. The first or left hand poster showed a person looking very depressed and suggesting that he suffered from a headache, the next or central poster showed the person taking a pill, and the last and final poster, on the right hand side showed a very happy person. The company executives manning the stand noticed bemused visitors who enquired why it was necessary to take pills in order to develop a headache.

Also read

- Advertising
- Signs, pictorial representations, emoticons and other symbols
- Verbal and visual presentations

TRAVELLING

Most countries have a well developed public or private transport infrastructure including aircraft, helicopters, railways and underground railways, buses, trams, taxis, human-powered and bicycle rickshaws, also lake, sea and river buses and boats. There are other countries that have just a few of these modes of transport, while yet others have virtually none.

Those who live in Western style societies are used to roads, streets and other thoroughfares having names or numbers or single letters of the alphabet by which they can be identified. Numbers and occasionally names are then used to identify individual buildings. This is not however a universal practice all over the world and there are still countries where only a few streets have a name or designation and where hardly any buildings are numbered. In some countries addresses are only identified by the name of a major building such as International House, or a particular hotel. A considerable degree of ingenuity on the part of a visitor may be called for in order to reach his destination and keep an appointment. In Tokyo, for example, only a handful of streets have names. Instead addresses are expressed using the name of the area, followed by three numbers representing the district, the block and the building.

Even when reaching one's destination, one could still be faced with some problems in locating an organization within a building, since the expression used to describe the street or ground level of a building is not universal in all countries, it is sometimes called ground floor and sometimes the first floor. The next floor above this level might be called first floor or mezzanine floor, or even the second floor. The text or icons on call buttons in lifts illustrate the floor levels in buildings. Acronyms may sometimes be used on lift call buttons. In France, for example, the ground floor button might display the letters 'RdC' (*Rez-de-Chaussée* or Ground Floor).

In a number of European countries including Austria, Germany and the Czech Republic 'paternoster lifts' are still in use. They move slowly up and down inside a building without stopping and one can step on or off at any level. Anyone not familiar with this type of lift might, at least initially, be uneasy about using it.

It is important that factors such as religious and secular holidays, annual holidays and climatic factors should be taken into consideration when planning to visit a foreign country.

In most countries there is only one time zone in operation and therefore train, bus, ship and airline timetables all indicate national or local time. This is very different in those countries which have more than one time zone. In the USA, which has seven time zones, air and train timetables usually quote the local time. In Russia however, which has eleven time zones, the whole of its rail network operates on Moscow time. And applies both to railway timetables and station clocks. The exception to this are suburban rail services which operate on local time.

In many countries it is obligatory for everybody to carry some legal form of identification such as an identity card or passport when outside their home, office or hotel, whilst in others like the United Kingdom there is no such requirement.

In many countries possession of unusual substances such as illegal drugs is a punishable offence. One should be aware of this if one is travelling with any form of unusual substances. Under this heading may fall personal medication, jet-lag tablets, powdered tea or even biological washing powder. If one is carrying unusual medication which could be mistaken for illegal drugs it is usually advisable to carry a doctor's prescription.

In some countries the reaction and response of the law enforcement agencies such as the police may be capricious or unpredictable when loss of property or an offence against a person is reported to them.

Also read

- Appointments
- Measuring and managing time
- Sex

Units of Measure

The units of measure are used to express and describe weight, volume, capacity, mass, size, speed, length, distance, area, time, temperature and humidity. They are based either on the decimal or the metric system or on a wide range of non-metric systems. There are countries where both the metric and the non-metric systems are used, for instance where linear measures are expressed in kilometres and metres, and at the same time the non-metric inch may still be used for engineering and various other purposes.

A wide range of different units of measure are in current use worldwide for describing paper size, formats, for measuring the speed of ships and aircraft, and for describing the capacity or size of Champagne bottles.

The gallon, pint and fluid ounce are used as a non-metric measurement of capacity by both the United States and the United Kingdom and although they bear the same name they are not of the same fluid capacity. The American gallon and pint are smaller than the British or Imperial gallon and pint, but the American fluid ounce is about 4% larger than the British fluid ounce. There are other instances of similar or almost similar terms being used, for example ton, short ton, metric ton and tonne all of which represent different units of weight.

There is now a wide range of internationally recognised standards, systems and conventions, in particular the International System of Units or SI which are applicable to measurement conversions. The SI takes in practically all units of measurement to be found around the world. The SI system also covers abbreviations and prefixes.

One should however be aware that even the SI symbols may not always be understood nor be capable of reproduction on some printing equipment in some languages.

Additionally there are other, often unusual, units of measure which are sometime used by the press and others to try to illustrate more clearly a unit of measure. These range from the practical to the bizarre and include something being 'x-times' the length of a (London) double-decker bus to give an indication of the length of an item, also something being 'x-times' the height of a double-decker bus. Another unit of measure sometimes used by the British media is to suggest that the area of an object is x-times the size a football pitch. Among some computer enthusiasts the word 'mickey' (for Mickey Mouse), is used to define the length of the smallest detectable movement of a computer mouse, the equivalent of $1/200^{th}$ of an inch.

Also read

- Information, operating instructions and methods of use
- Measuring and managing time

USING PROVERBS

It was the English philosopher and statesman Francis Bacon who wrote 'Genius, wit and spirit of a nation are discovered by their proverbs'. Every culture has a wealth of these and to be able to introduce an appropriate proverb at a suitable occasion can be most useful. One of the characteristics of proverbs can be the down-to-earth quality of their effect and impact.

In the context of not presuming to give advice to those who are more experienced and knowledgeable, the English proverb asserts 'to teach one's grandmother to suck eggs', in the Thai language the equivalent proverb states 'to teach a crocodile to swim'. The German proverb 'to make an elephant out of a mosquito' would in English be paraphrased into 'to make a mountain out of a molehill'.

It is however dangerous to translate proverbs literally rather than idiomatically. An advertisement was published by a European manufacturer in a South American country based on a well understood European proverb which showed a goose laying the proverbial 'golden egg'. However the local people could not understand the message at all, since in their country this practice is ascribed to hens.

In Italy one would touch *iron* for luck, whilst in England one would touch *wood*.

During a formal luncheon in Shanghai in China, the French-Canadian speaking mayor of Montreal made a point during his speech by saying 'Battre le fer quand il est chaud' by which he meant 'It is necessary to strike while the iron is hot'. Unfortunately the French-Canadian interpreter was not quite up to his task and translated this statement as 'You must beat your brother when he's drunk' or 'Battre son frere quand il est chaud'. The word 'chaud' being French-Canadian slang for 'drunk'.

Also read

- Jokes and anecdotes
- Sense of humour, laughter and smiles

VERBAL AND VISUAL PRESENTATIONS

When speaking to a foreign audience unless they, like the speaker also operate in a highly technical field, it is better to avoid idiomatic expressions and colloquialisms which are likely to cause problems for both the audience and, if used, interpreters. One should also speak more slowly than one would normally do, and unless one is using simultaneous interpretation, make one's presentation about half its normal duration.

Cultural factors influence listening and learning habits and this is reflected in the behaviour and attitude of audiences. It is therefore important for speakers to be aware of the customs and expectations of their prospective audience. In some countries there is a belief that taking copious notes during a lecture is an indicator of the attentiveness and interest of the audience. In some other countries the audience expects the presentation to be verbatim, that is word for word, from lecture manuscript, and it is not normal to take notes.

The posture which an audience expects to be adopted by a speaker is very much culture oriented, as are the nature of exchanges between speaker and audience. While there may be a highly vocal audience participation, including interruptions in some countries, in others an invitation to the audience to ask questions will be met with complete silence and it will only be later at smaller, private meetings with perhaps only a few of the participants at a time, that a lively discussion might take place.

Speakers should also be aware that in some countries, neither event organisers nor the audience acknowledge or accept the fact that the speaker will be able to answer questions from the floor on a spontaneous basis, even if the speaker happens to be a world authority on the subject. When invited to make presentation in these countries it is usually the practice to send the event organisers the full text of the presentation well ahead of the event. The organisers then distribute the full text to all those registered and enrolled for this event, together with an invitation for written questions. When questions have been received by the organisers they are sent to the speaker who prepares answers and returns these answers to the organisers well prior to the event. When the event finally takes place, the moderator or the person who initially asked the question, then reads out the question and the written answer is then read aloud by the speaker. Thereafter, sometimes but not often, this exchange may be followed by supplementary verbal questions.

The amount of text space requires modification when text is translated from one language into another. When something is translated from English into other Latin-based languages, approximately 20% to 25% more space may be required, and if translated into Arabic and Chinese probably 50% more.

If employing an interpreter it is important, whenever possible, to find a person who has some knowledge of the particular subject matter one is presenting and if possible also a native of the country where the presentation is taking place. If possible one should provide him with the full text or at the very least a summary of one's presentation, since this will assist him in putting one's points and ideas across more competently. If one cannot find an interpreter who has knowledge of the subject matter which one is presenting one should spend some time with him prior to the lecture to help with answers to any issues he may have, regarding any text or expressions with which he may not be familiar.

Visual presentations must take into account whether the audience or viewers read their language from left to right or right to left. There is the story of a poster advertising campaign for washing powder in a traditional Middle Eastern country. The campaign featured a number of posters — from left to right — from dirty clothes, through various stages of the washing using the product, to finally the clean clothes. It was only when sales dropped dramatically that advertising executives realised that the population whose language was Persian or Farsi, which like Arabic is read from right to left.

In voice-overs for television and video presentations and in recorded commentaries there are sometime misunderstandings and failures in communications caused by selecting inappropriate speakers, as there are many languages where cultural and nationality factors influence the way in which a language is spoken. This particularly applies to speakers who may have a strong regional dialect or use an uncommon form of a language usually spoken by members of a particular social or professional class.

It has been said that 'a language is a collection of mutually intelligible dialects.' Dialects are a variety or sub-division of a language and usually a regional or local language. Dialects take account of vocabulary, grammar and pronunciation. For example, the German language as spoken in most of Germany is generally understood in the neighbouring countries of Austria and Switzerland, on the contrary the Swiss-German dialect of 'Schweizerdeutsch' and the Austrian-German dialect, both a variety of the German language, are often not understood in Germany, except in border regions close to Austria or Switzerland. Likewise the Arabic spoken in Morocco is not the same as the Arabic spoken in the Arabian Gulf States.

When the English language is to be used for a presentation one should find out which variety of English is best understood by the audience and adjust one's presentation. There are many English words and expressions which are unlikely to be understood by English listeners and speakers in other countries, particularly so when English is not their mother tongue. It should be noted that there is standard English, as spoken in most of the regions of the United Kingdom, but there is also English as spoken in the United States, Canada, Australia, New Zealand and in Asia and South East Asia. Additionally there is also the functional English as used in the many countries in Europe, Africa, Asia and Central and South America. In the Indian Sub-Continent, for instance, a warehouse is known as 'godown' and eye glasses as 'opticals' and in North America one uses 'sidewalks' whilst in the United Kingdom one walks on pavements.

Also read

- Interpreting and translating
- Signs, pictorial representations, emoticons and other symbols
- Trade fairs and exhibitions

Visiting Other Countries

It may be obvious but it cannot be repeated too often that *it is the person who is visiting another country who is the foreigner.*

Many executives and visitors fail to make the appropriate mental adjustment, that it is not only *they* who are in a foreign land, but that it is 'they themselves who are foreigners in somebody else's homeland'. Visitors should note that it is the custom, as well as being more courteous, that it is they, the visitors who should make appropriate cultural adjustments and not their host.

There is the apocryphal story of an Englishman who was stopped for speeding in a small town in America and after a short conversation the American policeman asked 'Say are you a foreigner?', to which the indignant Englishman replied 'Certainly not, I'm British'.

Also read

- Courtesy

WOMEN IN BUSINESS AND THE PROFESSIONS

To anticipate how women executives are likely to be received and treated as potential business contacts or associates in another country it is advisable to be informed about the normal or day-to-day attitudes and manners in relation to women in that country. It has been suggest that to assist women executives to steer through the labyrinth of gender nuances in another country, particularly in male oriented societies, that it is not sufficient for them to rely upon their common sense. It is also necessary to fine-tune their antennae to increase their sense of perception. In practically all countries women still experience gender issues which include glass ceilings in their work and professions, they are, however, fewer than previous generations had to contend with.

It is prudent, prior to a female executive visiting another country to ascertain whether there are customs or conventions in regard to official, commercial, or professional activities being undertaken by women in that country. In many countries although people may appear to be progressive in their outlook there are still institutions and organisations as well as individuals who are deeply influenced by customs and practices based on traditional male-oriented conventions. Under such circumstances it is suggested that one takes steps, such as prior communication, to give an indication of the woman visitor's status and authority. In the absence of such action it might even be inappropriate for a woman either in a business or an official capacity to visit a country where the other party would expect for culture related reasons to meet a man.

There are many reasons for this state of affairs. The majority of today's organisations both religious and secular, including both commerce and the professions were created by men, for men. Within these organisations the concept of normal behaviour is the normal male behaviour and the normal career paths are the normal male career paths.

It has been suggested that when a professional or businesswoman finds herself in a male-oriented country or society where her arrival may appear to have resulted in culture shock, she might start off by saying — 'you may be wondering why a woman has been sent to deal with this affair or issue. It is because I am the expert in...'

Although there are circumstances where it would not be appropriate for Western culture organisations to send female executives do business in Muslim countries, there are other situations where it might well be advantageous. This would include the employment of female sales staff when wishing to be directly in touch with Muslim women, for example when seeking to sell cosmetics and clothes.

The division of labour between men and women is very much culture related. In practically every country and society there are a range of vocations, careers, professions and occupations which were and in some cases still are traditionally and customarily reserved either to men or to women. Never-the-less one should be aware that what may be considered conventional in one country may well be considered most strange or peculiar in another. Women are playing an ever increasingly active part in commercial and public life and in the professions in many countries where traditionally these functions were considered to be the exclusive preserve of men. Very often greater equality of sexes has been brought about by government policy. In some countries however, even at this point in time, attitudes are still old-fashioned and women's activities are still restricted to non-managerial functions. In some societies women are considered non-persons in the business and commercial sense, irrespective whether the woman concerned is the chief executive of a company or a receptionist. There are still countries where women are not permitted to drive, not even their own car.

Etiquette or conventions as to how single and married women are addressed either verbally or in writing vary from country to country. In English speaking countries for example this may include, in addition to Mrs and Miss, the term Ms. It is advisable to seek local advice about using the most appropriate title.

The custom prevailing in some countries of addressing married women by their husband's first name, for example Mrs John Brown, is not universal and in Germany for example, her own first name would be included, for example Frau Helga Braun. In many countries, married women, although they have assumed their husband's name, retain their maiden name in their professional capacity.

In the United States social skills training has focussed on assertiveness, this is thought to reflect general agreement and aspiration to become assertive. It has been found that this interest in forcefulness is strong in American women, as part of the women's lobby group. It manifests itself by frequently standing up for one's rights.

In Japan women are brought up to speak a feminine form of Japanese which has traditionally been used to institutionalise their different identity.

Conventions regarding the appropriateness of outer clothing or dress for women are not always the same as for men, particularly in Muslim countries, where women are subject to dress codes, which vary in their interpretation from country to country. In some of these countries where the role of women is still very circumscribed, a woman walking bareheaded in the street might well be described by zealous preachers as being naked, and it would even be considered sinful for anyone to talk to the husband who permits his wife to walk around in such a manner.

The following comment was made by a successful lady entrepreneur in connection with her professional activities in the financial sector: 'I actually think it is an advantage to be a women. Women probably relate to people a little bit differently, than men. They are more likely to listen and try and identify with the client in order to better understand what their situation is'.

Also read

- Dress code and etiquette
- Forms of address and use of titles
- Greeting, introductions, modes of address and leave-taking
- Male-female relationship
- Names

Summary

Confucius (551 BC – 479 BC) once said: 'By nature, men are nearly alike — by practice, they get to be wide apart.'

It is worthwhile noting that most governments take steps the ensure that their diplomats have some understanding of the history of the country to which they are posted. This ensures that they will arrive with a better understanding of the various issues and events that have shaped that country and provide an insight into the customs and beliefs of its people. As a result these diplomats may also be more perceptive to the character of its people and the passions and feelings which may agitate them.

Is it possible to be too concerned trying to cope with the many issues of cross-cultural relations? This is a question that may well spring to the mind of the person reading this book. It is a very relevant question. There is little doubt that if one becomes too preoccupied with the seemingly limitless possibilities for misinterpreted behaviour and as a result pays too little attention to the main purpose or object for visiting a foreign country, one has probably gone too far. There is no simple answer and ultimately common sense must be one's guide.

Even in wide-ranging observations like those in this book there may well be oversights and omissions, since it is clearly impossible to include every aspect of cross-cultural relations. It should also be remembered that culture, like most features of life, is subject to change and that some of the information might have been overtaken by events which in turn may have modified or changed cultural patterns. Finally, as in any kind of human activity, this book may also contain errors and for these I apologise.

END

About the author

Frederick Marsh is a well-known and experienced figure in industry, commerce and management consultancy. He has travelled extensively throughout the globe, visiting more than 90 countries.

He founded his consultancy company in 1975 and undertook management consultancy and market research projects, worldwide. His clients included many European companies and trans-national corporations, chambers of commerce, universities and management colleges, in particular the United Nations Geneva-based agency ITC-UNCTAD/ WTO and the Trade Development Institute of the Helsinki School of Economics.

He was a keynote speaker at many marketing seminars, which included cross-cultural presentations, and has written numerous articles on a wide range of topics for over 150 British and international trade publications.

He is President of the Royal Aero Club Trust, a registered charity. He was also the Founder President of Europe Airsports, the federation of all European aero clubs representing the interests of some 900,000 air sportsmen. He was the United Kingdom vice president of the FAI (Fédération Aéronautique Internationale), of which he is now a Companion of Honour. He is also a former air racing pilot and was British Air Racing Champion in 1972.

Since his retirement in 2005 his interests have stretched to include golf croquet, lawn bowling, watercolour painting, Scottish dancing and playing bridge.

Your suggestions and recommendations

We value all the comments we receive from readers.
Any suggestions and recommendations are welcome.
The author would be particularly pleased to receive personal cross-cultural anecdotes, gaffes and indiscretions.

Please mark all letters 'Social Kissing, Gifts and Bribes' and send to:

Indepenpress Publishing Limited
25 Eastern Place
Brighton
BN2 1GJ

Emails should be sent to:
info@penpress.co.uk